TO G —
With much love
H

THE POEMS OF

J. V. CUNNINGHAM

THE POEMS OF
J. V. CUNNINGHAM

EDITED WITH AN
INTRODUCTION &
COMMENTARY BY
TIMOTHY STEELE

SWALLOW PRESS / OHIO UNIVERSITY PRESS // ATHENS

Swallow Press/Ohio University Press, Athens, Ohio 45701
© 1942, 1947, 1950, 1957, 1960, 1964, 1965, 1967, 1971,
1973, 1983, 1988, 1997 by Jessie Cunningham
Introduction and Commentary © 1997 by Timothy Steele
Printed in the United States of America
All rights reserved. Published 1997

Swallow Press/Ohio University Press books are printed on acid-free paper ∞

01 00 99 98   5 4 3 2

Frontispiece: Photograph by Thomas Victor
Book design by Chiquita Babb

Library of Congress Cataloging-in-Publication Data

Cunningham, J.V. (James Vincent), 1911–
    [Poems, Selections]
    The poems of J.V. Cunningham / edited with an introduction and
commentary by Timothy Steele.
        p.   cm.
    Includes bibliographical references and index.
    ISBN 0-8040-0997-X (cloth : alk. paper). — ISBN 0-8040-0998-8
(pbk.)
    I Steele, Timothy. II. Title.
    PS3505.U435A17 1997
811'.54—dc21   97-355
                                                        CIP

Acknowledgments

Many people helped me while I was assembling this book. They include Jessie Campbell Cunningham, Jack Hagstrom, Rebecka Lindau, Paul G. Naiditch, Terry Santos, James Sullivan, Jerry Vanley, and Janet Lewis Winters. From their own libraries, R. L. Barth, Joshua Odell, and Luke O'Neill lent or photocopied for me rare items by or related to Cunningham. Bradin Cormack, Dick Davis, Ruben Quintero, Mark Salzman, and Helen Pinkerton Trimpi all read an early version of the introduction and contributed valuable suggestions for its improvement. Additional debts are owed to Professor Quintero and Dr. Trimpi for their unfailing kindness in discussing with me Cunningham's intellectual and biographical background. I am grateful to my wife Victoria for her patience during the time that this project absorbed me. For suggesting the project in the first place, and for encouraging me along the way to its completion, I thank David Sanders, the director of Ohio University Press/Swallow Press. And I thank Nancy Basmajian of Ohio/Swallow for her careful copy-editing of the book. Finally, I wish to express deep gratitude to the late Charles Gullans. Charles was perhaps Cunningham's most devoted and knowledgeable reader; and the assistance that Charles's bibliography of Cunningham's writings has given me may be inferred from the many references that my commentary makes to it.

Needless to say, those who have aided me are not responsible for the choices and judgments that this book reflects or expresses, much less for the errors that it may contain.

Timothy Steele

Contents

The Judge Is Fury (1947)

Doctor Drink (1950)

Introduction

Time will assuage.
Time's verses bury
Margin and page
In commentary,

For gloss demands
A gloss annexed
Till busy hands
Blot out the text . . .

ANYONE WHO EDITS J. V. Cunningham's work will be reminded of these lines from his poem "To the Reader." For the present editor, the reminder cuts keenly. Having long loved Cunningham's poetry—and hoping that this book will win him new admirers—I am reluctant to saddle his texts with apparatus that might deflect attention from their virtues. This reluctance is all the stronger on account of the body of Cunningham's verse being small. Introductory and exegetical materials must bulk even more intrusively here than they would in the cases of other poets. If I had my druthers, I would forgo critical comment and annotation altogether and would simply present Cunningham's poems to their audience with the succinct encouragement that Augustine heard: "Take up and read."

Such a course, however, would ill serve Cunningham. One of the finest and liveliest American poets of the twentieth century, he is underrated and misperceived. Although he enjoyed during his life a quiet but solid reputation among fellow poets, he was never fashionable. Anthologies and critical histories slighted or overlooked his contributions, and this neglect deepened when his work slipped out of print following his death in 1985. More to the point, the dominant poetic theories and practices of his time and ours have produced a literary community largely ignorant of the traditions that supported him and of the style in which he wrote. Explaining that style and those traditions may enable readers who might otherwise be nonplussed by him to appreciate his aims and achievements.

Explanatory materials will benefit Cunningham's work in more specific ways as well. For one thing, some of his earlier poems are obscure and require elucidation. He himself recognized this problem and wrote an autocritical essay, entitled "The Quest of the Opal," in which he endeavored to illuminate difficult passages in those poems. (The notes to this volume incorporate remarks from that essay.) For another thing, commentary is needed to bring back into focus particular frames of reference that have been blurred by the passage of time and changes in education. When Cunningham began publishing in the 1930s, he could assume that his audience had a reasonably sure hold of classical mythology and that it knew at least a handful of the more celebrated lyrics of antiquity. But some of today's readers, unless they have glosses, may have trouble following Cunningham when, for instance, he alludes to Iö and Danaë or when, in his elegy for a cricket, he rings thematic and metrical changes on Catullus's lament for Lesbia's sparrow.

What is more, the very nature of this book asks for an orienting context. Except for a limited-edition chapbook that appeared shortly after Cunningham's death, this is the first posthumous collection of his poems. And it is the most comprehensive collection ever. In view of these circumstances, it is only fitting to give the reader some sense of the poet's biography and his development as a writer, as well as of the ideas and themes that attracted or preoccupied him.

Cunningham's Life

Cunningham was born in Cumberland, Maryland on August 23, 1911. He was one of four children of working-class Irish-Catholic parents. In the mid-teens, his father, a steam-shovel operator who worked for the railroads, moved the family to Billings, Montana; and Montana and the railroads made profound impressions on the young Cunningham. Later in life, he would depict, in a number of his poems, the austere beauties of the American West and its lonely open spaces crossed by the trains. Further, he would always consider himself a native of Montana. More than forty years after he had last lived there, he introduced a lecture at Mount Holyoke on Emily Dickinson by saying apologetically: "I am a renegade Irish Catholic from the plains of Montana.... Consequently, I speak without authority on a nineteenth-century New England spinster."[1] On another occasion, commenting in the third person on his own writing, he referred to "his early life on the Montana plains" and noted that "he found that the patterns of his deepest feelings were most often clothed in the landscapes of that time" (CE, 414).

In 1923, at the insistence of Cunningham's mother, who was concerned about obtaining the best possible education for her children, the family moved to Denver. There Cunningham enrolled in the Jesuit-run Regis High School and took a rigorous curriculum that included four years of Latin and two of Greek. Having skipped two grades in the schools in Billings, he graduated in 1927, at age fifteen. The year before, however, Cunningham's father had been killed while working in California on the San Pedro harbor; his steam shovel had toppled over on an incline and crushed him. After his father's death, financial constraints apparently prevented Cunningham at that time from continuing his academic studies, except for a semester at St. Mary's College in Kansas.

In his late teens, Cunningham worked as a copyboy for the *Denver Morning Post* and then as a "runner"— a messenger/office boy—for Otis and Company, the largest brokerage house on the Denver Stock Exchange. And in 1929, while he was working for Otis, there occurred what he termed "the dominant experience of my life."[2] On October 29—Black Tuesday—the market crashed. "The day had a finality, inarguable, absolute," Cunningham recollected later, "though in fact the day seemed not to end. The ticker tape ran on past midnight Mountain Time, we slept a few hours in office chairs, and were back at work at 8 a.m."[3] Scarcely less traumatic was the aftermath of the crash. Cunningham particularly recalled the suicides of two of its victims:

> One [was] in the large lobby of the Equitable Building, filled with people. I'd come back from a run, paused a moment before going into the office, and casually looked across the lobby, all the way across. A man put a gun to his temple, and you heard the shot. Perhaps a day or two later, I was in the corridor, waiting for a call, when a body landed on the skylight within ten or fifteen feet of where I was standing.[4]

Cunningham soon found himself, like so many others, unemployed. With his older brother, he set off on a year of wandering through the Southwest, trying to eke out a living by freelance writing for trade journals of the day—business magazines, such as *Dry Goods Economist* and *The American Lumberman*. This work was even less profitable than it sounds. Cunningham and his brother made little money and were intermittently homeless. There was, as Cunningham said of this period, "a good deal of starving involved."[5]

In 1931, Cunningham wrote from temporary lodgings in Tucson to the poet Yvor Winters, then a graduate student and instructor at Stanford University. Cunningham had earlier corresponded with Winters about poetry, and on this occasion he explained his plight to Winters and asked "if it was possible to go to college and stay alive."[6] Winters immediately wrote back, urging Cunningham to come to California. When Cunningham arrived, Winters and his wife, Janet Lewis, put him up in a cottage/shed behind their house. Cunningham enrolled at Stanford, majoring in classics as an undergraduate and eventually receiving his doctorate in English for a dissertation on Shakespeare.[7]

Because a fair amount of misinformation has been written about Cunningham's relationship with Winters, a few words on the subject are in order. Cunningham regarded Winters as a man of immense personal generosity, and Winters's timely kindness enabled Cunningham to recover from privations that had nearly destroyed him. Given the opportunity to continue his education, he never looked back. Nonetheless, the two men clashed almost as soon as they met, and their friendship was frequently strained. This tension resulted from various causes, a couple of which can be mentioned here.

The first is that both men had strong and decided personalities. Problems inevitably arose. These were exacerbated, Cunningham felt in retrospect, by Winters's sometimes overbearing manner and by Cunningham's poor physical and mental shape. This made him, he suspected, overreact when he believed, as he did occasionally, that Winters was trying to establish intellectual primacy in their friendship.[8]

A second factor concerns aesthetics. Cunningham and Winters shared a belief in the value of intelligence; they shared the view that fine art blends subjective experience with objective structure, each enlivening and transforming the other. Yet in terms of particular styles and proclivities, they differed widely. To use an inadequate but not inaccurate contrast, Winters was more a romantic and Cunningham more a classicist. Winters's poetry centrally concerns the natural world and draws on the particulars of his experience; and while Winters criticized elements of romanticism and modernism, he began his career as an Imagist and late in life believed even more strongly in the Imagist idea that well-rendered sensory detail could convey conceptual content. His theory of "post-Symbolism" is in one respect an attempt at a richer and more intellectually complex version of Imagism. Cunningham's poetry, on the other hand, inclines to logical statement and syllogistic argument; and he seems at times to doubt the efficacy of the details that one finds in some of Winters's verse and much other modern poetry. For example, in his essay "The Journal of John Cardan," Cunningham argues that poems dealing with "passion, evil, or social mischance" have merit only "in the generality of application to others, and in private surmise to the hearer's self. But realistic detail impedes this effect, localizes the general in the particular places, times, and persons concerned" (*CE,* 426).

Cunningham admired fine poems in the Romantic tradition, such as Keats's "To Autumn," Stevens's "Sunday Morning," and Winters's "Summer Commentary." Yet he distrusted the vatic and personal elements in much romantic and modern poetry, Winters's included. Winters, by the same token, admired Cunningham's precise use of abstractions, just as he could admire the intellectual verse of Fulke Greville or Ben Jonson. But he considered some of Cunningham's verse to be elliptical and under-realized. Over the years, the two poets launched a number of zingers at each other. For example, it was with Winters in mind that Cunningham spoke of his "early associates who were almost without exception congenital romantics, however classical their creed" (*CE,* 406); and when Winters at the end of "The Manzanita" exclaimed of the forest, "There is no wisdom here," Cunningham commented: "I never thought there was."[9] For his part, Winters wrote of Cunningham's "Agnosco Veteris Vestigia Flammae" that the poem "would be very moving if one could imagine the experience"; and Winters added generally: "Cunningham is seldom perceptive of the physical universe around him; he does not know what to do with it."[10]

Contrary to what has been reported, Cunningham was never Winters's student. They were friends and colleagues. To repeat, Winters was a graduate student and instructor when Cunningham arrived at Stanford. Winters did not receive his doctorate until 1934, and not until 1937 was he appointed an assistant professor in the English Department at the school, by which time Cunningham was well along in his own graduate work.

The truth is that Winters and Cunningham shared a teacher, William Dinsmore Briggs. Briggs was a Renaissance scholar, and he figured pivotally in the lives of both pupils. Winters seems to have elected, even before he attended Stanford, to devote his prose to literary criticism; nothing that occurred at Stanford altered this decision. But Briggs interested Winters in scholarship and gave him a respect for it; and Briggs encouraged in Winters a concern with the history of ideas that lent a depth to his work that it would not have had otherwise. As for Cunningham, Briggs sparked his interest in Renaissance lyric and in the Renaissance revival of the classical plain style—interests that helped to focus Cunningham's own gifts as a writer. Cunningham's admiration and serious study of Jonson, it might be added, date from a summer in graduate school when Briggs became ill and asked Cunningham to pinch-hit for him in his seminar on the poet. (Briggs's academic specialty was Jonson, and he had hoped to do an edition of him, but C. H. Herford and Percy and Evelyn Simpson got to the job first.) Both Cunningham and Winters publicly expressed gratitude to Briggs. Winters wrote two poems to him—and a third about him—and Cunningham dedicated his study of Shakespearean tragedy, *Woe or Wonder,* to his memory.

Cunningham did not take his doctorate until 1945. Part of the reason is that World War II broke out, and Cunningham for a time taught mathematics to pilots at The Seventh Army Air Base at Santa Ana in southern California. (All his life, he was interested in mathematics, and he treated mathematical topics in such poems as "Meditation on Statistical Method" and his epigram on Georg Cantor.) Following the war, and after completing his doctorate, Cunningham held a series of teaching posts at the Universities of Hawaii, Chicago, Harvard, and Virginia. In 1953, he was hired by Brandeis University, where he taught until his retirement in 1980. If he felt deep personal debts to such individuals as Winters, Briggs, and Morris Rosenfeld (the owner of a bookstore in Denver who encouraged the teenaged Cunningham's interest in modern literature), he felt a great professional affection for Brandeis. Not long before his death, he commented on the irony of an Irish-Catholic Westerner's finding a home in an institution created principally by the energies of the Jewish community on the East Coast.

Cunningham was married three times: from 1937 to 1942 to the poet Barbara Gibbs; from 1945 to 1949 to Dolora Gallagher, like Cunningham a scholar of Shakespeare and the Renaissance; and from 1950 until his death to Jessie MacGregor Campbell, a scholar of Jane Austen and nineteenth-century fiction. Cunningham had one child, a daughter by his first marriage. For the last thirty years of his life, he lived in Sudbury, Massachusetts. He died of heart failure, brought on in part by emphysema and a hip fracture, on March 30, 1985, at Marlborough Hospital in Marlborough, Massachusetts.

Cunningham's Poems

We can chart precisely Cunningham's development as a poet, thanks to Charles Gullans's *Bibliography of the Published Works of J. V. Cunningham.*[11] When Gullans compiled the bibliography, Cunningham noted for him the place and date of composition for most of the poems. Gullans lists this information in an appendix to the bibliography.

One of the miracles of Cunningham's best work is that it says so much so well in so little space; some of his early poems, however, are overly dense. They need more words than they have. Any writer who aims for compression, as Cunningham does, risks becoming so concise as to be impenetrable. As Horace says in *The Art of Poetry* (25–26),

> I seek sound style, but my grasp isn't sure:
> Striving for brevity, I grow obscure.[12]

This matter is doubly tricky for a poet like Cunningham, who often works in short metrical lines, such as trimeters and dimeters. Any metrical line encourages grammatical compactness; when poets write in brief measures, the pressure for verbal economy is even more acute. And they may be tempted, particularly when young and inexperienced, to suppress functional words and phrases that have little intrinsic attraction but may be essential in relating images or arguments. This temptation is all the more seductive because, under certain conditions, no figure of speech is more effective in verse than *asyndeton*—"unconnectedness" —the startling or agitated juxtaposition of phrases, ideas, images.

In "The Quest of the Opal," Cunningham notes another source of difficulty in some of his early poems: "the use . . . of special learning and uncommon reference" (*CE,* 407). That is, on occasion Cunningham will allude to esoteric philosophical issues, and only those who share the poet's knowledge of the issues will be able to grasp his meaning.

The liabilities of both special learning and grammatical compression may be illustrated by the second stanza of Cunningham's "The Beacon":

> The will in pure delight
> Conceives itself. I praise
> Far lamps at night,
> Cold landmarks for reflection's gaze.

These lines appear to allude to the scholastic distinction between Reason— selfless and transcendental—and Will—selfish and solipsistic. Cunningham discusses this distinction in *Woe or Wonder.* Here, however, the distinction is only implied. Just one of the terms—"the will"—is stated, nor is its negative nature clearly indicated. Indeed, merely conceiving something in pure delight sounds like a relatively harmless intellectual activity. And reading the stanza cold, one might think that its second sentence follows from the first and that the will is being lauded, or that its conceptualizing capacity is connected with "reflection's gaze," or that the will's being delighted results in its bursting forth with praise. But in fact the two sentences stand in diametric opposition. Cunningham might have clarified the nature of the will by saying something like, "The will in pure delight / Wants to get drunk," but this would have been a tonal lapse. Or he could have begun the second sentence with a "But" or "Yet." The meter, though, won't allow another syllable there. Consequently, one has to struggle to get the point.

It is interesting to compare to the stanza the gloss that Cunningham gives it in "The Quest of the Opal." He writes, "[T]he will takes pleasure in begetting its own image. I on the contrary choose an object other and distant, a cold land-mark toward which contemplation looks. . . . [T]he will is delighted to beget it-self. Hence we must reserve prestige for the external and the distant, the distinct and the remote" (*CE,* 413–14). These remarks clarify the negative nature of the will and the relationship of the two sentences. The gloss is intelligible because it spells out the philosophical issue and contains a conjunctive phrase, "on the contrary," that supplies a crucial transition absent from the poem.

As Cunningham matured, he grew more adept at harmonizing metrical in-tegrity and grammatical cogency. He acquired, too, greater tact in deploying his learning: he developed a surer sense of when and when not to draw on it in his verse. But, as is the case with most poets, it took time for Cunningham to de-velop these skills.

Despite occasional obscurities, Cunningham's early work is interesting and features such wonderfully successful poems as "Poets survive in fame," "Timor Dei," "The Symposium," and "Montana Pastoral." Further, the early poems as a group comprise a narrative that illuminates Cunningham's subsequent develop-ment. As Cunningham says in "The Quest of the Opal," when he compiled his first collection, *The Helmsman,* the poems "were arranged roughly in chrono-logical order, and hence there was in the successive poems of the book a story. . . . It could be told as well in technical terms as in dramatic; it could be regarded as the history of a style" (*CE,* 407). In this respect, *The Helmsman* is like Robert Frost's first book, *A Boy's Will.* Each chronicles, however reticently, a coming-of-age and the disappointments and affirmations that issue from that process.

The "technical" aspect of the quest in the early poems involves the attempt, on Cunningham's part, to be a modern poet, as that term was then understood. Cunningham was seeking, he tells us, to write a poetry expressive of "sensibil-ity: the province of modern art, the deep well of creativity, the secret and sacred recesses of personality, the Gothic chamber of modern psychology, and the fall of light among the teacups" (*CE,* 410). In considering this objective, we should remember that Cunningham, regardless of his classical training and natural bent, grew up in the heyday of modernism and explored it when it still was genuinely modern. While yet in his teens in Denver, he read the fiction of D. H. Lawrence and James Joyce and purchased copies of Wallace Stevens's *Harmonium,* William Carlos Williams's *Spring and All,* and Mina Loy's *Lunar Baedeker.* And while an undergraduate at Stanford, he contributed prose and verse to such cutting-edge journals as *Hound and Horn.* However skeptical of modernism, he studied it carefully. And in a number of poems in *The Helmsman,* such as the jaggedly cin-ematic "Wandering Scholar's Prayer to St. Catherine of Egypt," he endeavored to see to what extent he might use the oblique and fragmented methods of the modernists.

The "dramatic" aspect of the early poems involves the pursuit of love. Cunningham does not, in "The Quest of the Opal," speak of this element explicitly, but a reader of the poems can sense it. And if one knows the poet's biography, one can see in the poems reflections of the trials and eventual breakup of his first marriage.

These two pursuits—the quest for sensibility and the quest for love—are memorably conflated in "The Dogdays." Though written in 1932, the poem, as Cunningham remarked subsequently, "may be regarded not only as anticipatory of the undetermined future, but almost as an epilogue, a summary after the event, detailing the plot [of *The Helmsman*]" (*CE*, 411). The poem conveys a desolate feeling of promises unfulfilled and explorations that did not produce hoped-for discoveries.

> The morning changes in the sun
> As though the hush were insecure,
> And love, so perilously begun,
> Could never in the noon endure,
>
> The noon of unachieved intent,
> Grown hazy with unshadowed light,
> Where changing is subservient
> To hope no longer, nor delight.
>
> Nothing alive will stir for hours,
> Dispassion will leave love unsaid,
> While through the window masked with flowers
> A lone wasp staggers from the dead.
>
> Watch now, bereft of coming days,
> The wasp in the darkened chamber fly,
> Whirring ever in an airy maze,
> Lost in the light he entered by.

The quest, then, failed. The love died, and, to speak of the technical side of the pursuit, Cunningham discovered that he was not a poet suited to the modes with which he had been experimenting. The darkened room of romance and sensibility proved a labyrinth.

As unhappy as this outcome was, acknowledging it enabled Cunningham to move on. *The Helmsman* was published in 1942, which was also the year that his first marriage ended in divorce. Thereafter, he hit his stride as a poet. He moved into that gracefully logical and urbane manner that he would employ for the remainder of his life. If there is a narrowing of stylistic focus, his poems gain depth, concentration, and accessibility. Between 1942 and 1944, he wrote many of his best and most distinctive poems, including "Ars Amoris," "Meditation on Statistical Method," "To the Reader," and "Meditation on a Memoir." In addition, he began to explore the epigram. (Only seven epigrams appear in *The Helmsman,* and five of these were written in 1940–1941, shortly before the collection appeared. In contrast, forty-three epigrams would appear in his next book.) And many of Cunningham's most memorable epigrams—"Deep summer, and time pauses," "Within this mindless vault," "Hang up your weaponed wit," and "This Humanist"—date from 1942 to 1944.

Cunningham gathered these and other materials (including a few early poems that had not made it into *The Helmsman)* into his second collection of verse, *The Judge Is Fury.* Published in 1947, this is probably the high-water mark of Cunningham's poetry. The collection shows to fine advantage Cunningham's talents both at conventional poems and at epigrams. Following this book, he turned increasingly to the epigram. Even in the narrative sequence that he published in 1964, *To What Strangers, What Welcome,* five of the fifteen poems are epigrammatic.

Conditions in Cunningham's life may have contributed to the increasing prominence of the epigram in his work. To be sure, he had a natural affinity for the genre and felt an almost metabolic bond with it. He once remarked: "I am, so to speak, a short-breathed man, and simply found that I had an almost unthought-out preference for brief definitiveness of statement, so that there was a traditional form just waiting for me to find it."[13] Yet also, in the late 1940s and early 1950s, Cunningham was teaching full-time and was publishing quite a bit of prose. *Woe and Wonder* appeared in 1951, and, during the same period, he wrote for journals most of the essays that he collected in 1960 in *Tradition and Poetic Structure.* Though his poems are rarely longer (and are often shorter) than twenty lines, they demanded an argumentative development not required by the epigrams, which Cunningham could and sometimes did compose mentally, writing them down only when he had completed and subjected them to final tinkering. And he may have moved more and more in the direction of epigrams because they could be conceived and shaped at odd moments in the day or during travels.

Cunningham published several small limited editions of verse in the 1950s move on. *The Helmsman* was published in 1942, which was also the year that his first marriage ended in divorce. Thereafter, he hit his stride as a poet. He moved into that gracefully logical and urbane manner that he would employ for the remainder of his life. If there is a narrowing of stylistic focus, his poems gain depth, concentration, and accessibility. Between 1942 and 1944, he wrote many of his best and most distinctive poems, including "Ars Amoris," "Meditation on Statistical Method," "To the Reader," and "Meditation on a Memoir." In addition, he began to explore the epigram. (Only seven epigrams appear in *The Helmsman,* and five of these were written in 1940–1941, shortly before the collection appeared. In contrast, forty-three epigrams would appear in his next book.) And many of Cunningham's most memorable epigrams—"Deep summer, and time pauses," "Within this mindless vault," "Hang up your weaponed wit," and "This Humanist"—date from 1942 to 1944.

Cunningham gathered these and other materials (including a few early poems that had not made it into *The Helmsman)* into his second collection of verse, *The Judge Is Fury.* Published in 1947, this is probably the high-water mark of Cunningham's poetry. The collection shows to fine advantage Cunningham's talents both at conventional poems and at epigrams. Following this book, he turned increasingly to the epigram. Even in the narrative sequence that he published in 1964, *To What Strangers, What Welcome,* five of the fifteen poems are epigrammatic.

Conditions in Cunningham's life may have contributed to the increasing prominence of the epigram in his work. To be sure, he had a natural affinity for the genre and felt an almost metabolic bond with it. He once remarked: "I am, so to speak, a short-breathed man, and simply found that I had an almost unthought-out preference for brief definitiveness of statement, so that there was a traditional form just waiting for me to find it."[13] Yet also, in the late 1940s and early 1950s, Cunningham was teaching full-time and was publishing quite a bit of prose. *Woe or Wonder* appeared in 1951, and, during the same period, he wrote for journals most of the essays that he collected in 1960 in *Tradition and Poetic Structure.* Though his poems are rarely longer (and are often shorter) than twenty lines, they demanded an argumentative development not required by the epigrams, which Cunningham could and sometimes did compose mentally, writing them down only when he had completed and subjected them to final tinkering. And he may have moved more and more in the direction of epigrams because they could be conceived and shaped at odd moments in the day or during travels.

Cunningham published several small limited editions of verse in the 1950s poems addressed to people close to him. For instance, the following epigram, written for his daughter, suggests that even the bond that parents feel with their offspring is qualified by the distinction and independence of the child:

> Dear child, whom I begot,
> Forgive me if my page
> Hymns not your helpless age,
> For you are mine, and not:
> Mine as sower and sown,
> But in yourself your own.

And this same idea is expressed in broader terms in "For a Woman with Child":

> We are ourselves but carriers. Life
> Incipient grows to separateness
> And is its own meaning. . . .

Because our own lives so intensely absorb us, we naturally incline to interpret others primarily with reference to our ideas and emotions, and one of the impressive things about Cunningham's treatment of otherness is that he always acknowledges the power of subjective experience. Yet his poems urge that we should bear in mind and heart that our friends, children, spouses, and siblings have their own perceptions of life and their own ways of responding to it. Nor should we imagine that we are truly concerned for them unless we are attentive to their being as well as to our experience of their being. Cunningham's most poignant expression of this idea is that passage in *To What Strangers, What Welcome* where the speaker says to his lover: "If I love you—as I do—/ . . . It's that I care more for you / Than for my feeling for you."

The importance of acknowledging otherness also appears, by contrary example, in several poems in which Cunningham depicts types of egotism. In "The Solipsist," for instance, Cunningham writes of the title character: "Others are you. Your *hence* / Is personal consequence; / Desire is reason." And in other poems, Cunningham portrays "Will" not only as something that can undermine intellect (as is the case in "The Beacon"), but also as something that can obliterate our concern with the external world and its claims. For instance, in "Ars Amoris," a poem about sexual egotism, Cunningham speaks bitterly of "Love's wilful potion"; and the same sentiment appears in his epigram on the famous lovers who drank that wilful potion and who consequently caused others so much suffering:

> Within this mindless vault
> Lie Tristan and Isolt

> Tranced in each other's beauties.
> They had no other duties.

Cunningham's concern with respecting others also reflects an awareness of the fragility of human identity. This awareness no doubt partly derives from his experience of the Depression and from seeing the bottoms drop out of so many lives overnight. Some of his early poems hint as well that he felt that aspects of his background at times threatened to consume him. "A Moral Poem," for example, indicates that the speaker must, to grow and develop in his own terms, "leave old regret, / Ancestral remorse," and must become "[i]nured to the past." And in "Timor Dei," Cunningham intimates that his religious heritage has become suffocating—indeed, that Divinity is itself menacing:

> Most beautiful, most dear,
> When I would use Thy light,
> Beloved, omniscient Seer,
> Thou didst abuse my sight;
>
> Thou didst pervade my being
> Like marsh air steeped in brine;
> Thou didst invade my seeing
> Till all I saw was Thine. . . .

In a different vein, the final poem of *To What Strangers, What Welcome* construes our bodies and lives as mere packets of physical-biochemical matter borrowed for a brief while from the universal energy bank:

> Identity, that spectator
> Of what he calls himself, that net
> And aggregate of energies
> In transient combination . . .

Accompanying this sense of the tenuousness of life is an alertness to the limits of our knowledge and our ability to understand even ourselves. This topic is explored in a number of epigrams—"I don't know what I am," "On a Line from Bodenham's 'Belvedere,'" and "Gnothi Seauton"—as well as in "Meditation on a Memoir," which begins

> Who knows his will?
> Who knows what mood
> His hours fulfil?
> His griefs conclude?

Particularly in Cunningham's earlier poems, one other theme figures prominently. It is that actuality diminishes potentiality. In this preoccupation, Cunningham resembles Frost, especially the Frost of such poems as "The Road Not Taken." Cunningham, however, explores the theme not in terms of two roads diverging in a yellow wood, but rather in relation to the concept of "haecceity," derived from the Latin word *haecceitas,* meaning "thisness." This concept much occupied medieval philosophers, for many of whom goodness was identical with realized being. In a poem that takes the word as its title, Cunningham states his radically modern view on the topic:

> Evil is any this or this
> Pursued beyond hypothesis. . . .

Or as Cunningham summarizes the matter in "The Quest of the Opal": "The more realized a thing is the greater its defect of being; hence any particular choice is as such evil though morally it may be the best choice" (*CE,* 412).

Cunningham's view of haecceity is fascinating. Psychologically and philosophically, he appears to have felt deeply threatened by choice and self-definition. Yet no one appreciated better than he the importance of choice, and no one committed himself more fiercely, loyally, and self-definedly to choices. Further, as a poet, he recognized that to write effectively one must select certain verbal possibilities and reject others; and, in reference to this process, he entitled one of his books *The Exclusions of a Rhyme.* Nevertheless, like the serpent in Paul Valéry's "Sketch of a Serpent," Cunningham at times clearly regretted those principles of being or nature that transform potentiality into actualization.

Possibly this attitude has something to do with Cunningham's loss of religious faith. If we believe in some form of God and believe that our specificity is encompassed by and related to Eternal Being, we can regard individuation positively. The fact that God can be everything frees us to realize our particular selves. If we lose faith, however, the immediacies of our existence become problematical and can lead to the concerns that we find in Cunningham and in so many other modern writers.

As striking as Cunningham's view of haecceity is, his poems on the subject— "All Choice Is Error," "How we desire desire," and "Agnosco Veteris Vestigia Flammae" are others—are not his most engaging. They entail a certain futile pessimism. In simple human terms, one can appreciate the wish to be or do all things; likewise, one can appreciate the longing to escape the multitude of limits and responsibilities that hedge our lives. Yet as Richard Wilbur observes in

"Seed Leaves"—a gentle comment on Frost that might be equally applied to Cunningham—every living thing must eventually become

> ... resigned
> To being self-defined
> Before it can converse
> With the great universe ...[16]

It is interesting that, in "The Metaphysical Amorist," Cunningham invokes Duns Scotus as a means of reconciling the idealism of Plato and the sensationalism of Hume. Scotus argued that real knowledge rested not only in abstract categories, but also in the immediate haecceity of things. Indeed, he contended that the distinction between the universal and the particular is merely "formal"(*distinctio formalis a parte rei*). We can mentally distinguish the two, but they are inseparable in reality. In a human being, for instance, the general humanity and the specific haecceity of the person are inextricably and simultaneously actual. Scotus did not see, that is, haecceity as "evil." So Cunningham may himself have been of two minds about the topic.[17]

This account of Cunningham's themes is necessarily incomplete since much of his poetry is satirical. As such, it does not take up and develop motifs, but rather analyzes conditions, situations, and temperaments that we all are likely to meet in the course of life. About this aspect of Cunningham, more will be said in the the concluding section of this introduction.

Cunningham and the Plain Style

Cunningham's style is at odds with assumptions that we commonly entertain about poetic speech. Many of us share the view set forth by *The Random House Dictionary of the English Language* (2nd ed.) when it speaks of "Poetry" as "lofty thought or impassioned feeling expressed in imaginative words." We expect, that is, that the diction of poetry will differ markedly from that of prose. We expect that the language of poems will be more figurative, perhaps, or more sensory. And we anticipate that poetry will feature, in association with its unusual verbal properties, an obvious intellectual or emotional urgency. Cunningham's poems, however, are relatively bare of ornament, and his mature verse, far from sounding unconventional, impresses instead by its colloquial directness and clarity. Further, though Cunningham's poems are serious, they are also clever and often are unabashedly humorous.

Cunningham, in brief, writes in "the plain style." This term refers to one of the three "modes of speech" *(genera dicendi)* of the ancient rhetorical tradition, the other two being the middle or pleasant and the high or grand. And briefly reviewing the history of the plain style will help us to understand Cunningham's own use of it.

The first thing to say about the plain style is that our English adjective gives but a poor sense of the original terms for and intentions of the style. In Greek, the words denoting the plain style are *ischnos* (e.g., Demetrius, *On Style,* 190),[18] meaning "lean, spare," and, less frequently, *leptos* (e.g., Dionysius of Halicarnassus, *Isocrates,* 3), meaning "fine, light, delicate." Though Roman writers introduce a wider range of terms for the style, the nearest Latin equivalent to *ischnos* and *leptos* is *subtilis;* and it is with this term that Cicero and Quintilian most often refer to the plain style. *Subtilis* derives from *subtexo* ("to weave beneath, to connect, to join") and means "subtle, discriminating, finely woven." Cunningham himself alludes to the word's etymological associations when he describes his own plain style as being "crisscrossed and webbed with subtlety and distinctions" *(CE,* 408). In other words, the plain style aims at nimble sophistication.

Among ancient writers, Cicero offers the most penetrating, sympathetic, and influential examination of the plain style. This circumstance is ironic, because Cicero was not a plain stylist. Indeed, he was criticized for extravagance by younger contemporaries who advocated reviving an "Attic" plainness of style and who wished to purge contemporary Roman oratory of "Asiatic" excesses. ("Asiatic" meant "showy" and referred to schools in the Greek islands and Greek Asia Minor, where an increasingly artificial approach to rhetoric had been adopted.) Cicero was skeptical of the Attic reformers, who included his good friend Brutus. Cicero took the sensible view that a writer or speaker should, ideally, command all styles, however unlikely it was that anybody save a second Homer could perfectly realize this ideal in practice. Yet at the same time Cicero believed that mastery of the plain style was essential for literary excellence. And because he also felt that the reformers misunderstood the plain style, and were substituting for it an overly severe manner of speech, he was eager to define what he considered the style's true qualities and virtues.

Because Cicero's discussion of the plain style is important to Cunningham (and for that matter many other English poets), I should like to quote from it in some detail. Of the plain stylist, Cicero writes (*Orator,* 76):

> [H]e follows the ordinary usage, really differing more than is supposed from those who are not eloquent at all. Consequently the audience, even if they are no speakers themselves, are sure they can speak in that fashion. For that plainness of

style (*orationis subtilitas*) seems easy to imitate at first thought, but when attempted nothing is more difficult.

And of the plain style itself, Cicero says (*Orator,* 78–81):

> It should be loose but not rambling; so that it may seem to move freely but not to wander without restraint. . . . For the short and concise clauses must not be handled carelessly, but there is such a thing even as a careful negligence. Just as some women are said to be handsomer when unadorned—this very lack of ornament becomes them—so this plain style (*subtilis oratio*) gives pleasure even when unembellished: there is something in both cases which lends greater charm, but without showing itself. Also all noticeable ornament, pearls as it were, will be excluded; not even curling irons will be used; all cosmetics, artificial white and red, will be rejected; only elegance and neatness will remain. . . . Consequently the orator of the plain style, provided he is elegant and finished, will not be bold in coining words, and in metaphor will be modest, sparing in the use of archaisms, and somewhat subdued in using other embellishments of language and of thought.

This discussion of the plain style clearly impressed Cunningham. When he edited an anthology entitled *The Problem of Style* (New York: Fawcett, 1966), he included both of these passages as well as other material from the *Orator.* He himself refers to the second passage when, in his introductory essay to the anthology, he discusses the potential pitfalls of any style that flamboyantly announces itself: "[I]f it fails it seems frigid, bombastic, artificial. . . . And so the problem arises of hedging against failure, employing the art that conceals art, or alternatively, of developing an unrhetorical plain style whose 'careful negligence' may yet permit distinction" (*CE,* 255). And he alludes to the first passage in a different essay, "Lyric Style in the 1590s," which discusses the revival of the classical plain style in the late Elizabethan period. Here he argues that up to that time English poets have at their disposal only three limited, unsatisfactory alternatives—a "sweet" style, a "moral" style, and a "flat" style—and he remarks of this situation: "What is needed is a noticeably unnoticeable style, the style of Cicero's Attic orator, *Nam orationis subtilitas imitabilis illa videtur esse existimanti, sed nihil est experienti minus,* 'a directness of speech that seems to one judging easily imitable, to one trying it nothing less so'" (*CE,* 322). It might be added that the sentence that Cunningham cites from Cicero well describes the effect of Cunningham's verse. Reading his epigrams, one imagines, "I could probably knock off a few of these." But once one tries to write something witty, exact, and complete in, say, a single iambic pentameter couplet, the task grows more demanding.

Cicero's discussion, it should also be observed, is repeatedly referred to by the Renaissance poets Cunningham studied with Briggs. Thomas Campion, for instance, draws on Cicero's discussion when, in "Thou art not fair, for all thy red and white, / For all those rosy ornaments in thee," he equates plain style in literature with sincerity in love. The same association occurs in several of Jonson's lyrics, such as "Still to Be Neat, Still to Be Dressed." And Cicero's analysis is the key source for George Herbert when he connects plainness of literary style with sincerity of religious worship in "Jordan I" ("Who says that fictions only and false hair / Become a verse," etc.) and in "Jordan II":

> When first my lines of heav'nly joys made mention,
> Such was their lustre, they did so excel,
> That I sought out quaint words, and trim invention;
> My thoughts began to burnish, sprout, and swell,
> Curling with metaphors a plain intention,
> Decking the sense as if it were to sell. . . .

Cunningham is Ciceronian in that he does not give the plain style the favorable moralistic constructions that one finds in such Renaissance works as Herbert's. In his criticism, Cunningham acknowledges that all styles have their legitimacy and advantages. Further, he is well aware that though the plain style can do some things it cannot do others and that it may in some circumstances prove ineffectual. He wrote a book, after all, on Shakespearean tragedy and knew that the death of the Roman Republic, at least according to Shakespeare's interpretation in *Julius Caesar,* resulted from a failure of the plain style. No orator was less purely Attic or more decadently Asiatic than Antony. As Plutarch says of Antony's literary studies and tastes (*Life of Antony,* 2.5): "He adopted what was called the Asiatic style of oratory *(Asianōi logōn),* which was at the height of its popularity in those days and bore a strong resemblance to his own life, which was swashbuckling and boastful, full of empty exultation and distorted ambition." But at Caesar's funeral, Antony's rhetoric, with its manipulative emotionalism, routed the honest scrupulosities of Brutus, the plain stylist. (Shakespeare turns the tables in *Antony and Cleopatra,* which examines, among other things, the liabilities of Antony's stylistic excesses: drunk as much on rhetoric as on romance, Antony entirely loses grip on the personal, political, and military realities around him.)[19]

Yet the plain style has the virtues of clarity, compression, and wit. Moreover, it has a self-sufficiency that the high style lacks. By itself it can do much, whereas the grand mode is suited only to occasions when pulling out all the stops is appropriate. Cicero summarizes the matter thus (*Orator,* 98-99):

One who has studied the plain and pointed style *(subtili et acuto)* so as to be able to speak adroitly and neatly, and has not conceived of anything higher, if he has attained perfection in this style, is a great orator, if not the greatest. He is far from standing on slippery ground, and, when once he gets a foothold, he will never fall. . . . But this orator of ours whom we consider the chief,—grand, impetuous and fiery, if he has natural ability for this alone, or trains himself solely in this, or devotes his energies to this only, and does not temper his abundance with the other two styles, he is much to be despised. For the plain orator is esteemed wise because he speaks clearly and adroitly; the one who employs the middle style is charming; but the copious speaker, if he has nothing else, seems to be scarcely sane. For a man who can say nothing calmly and mildly, who pays no attention to arrangement, precision, clarity or pleasantry . . . seems to be a raving madman among the sane, like a drunken reveller in the midst of sober men.

These points are relevant to Cunningham. The plain is hardly the only style, nor is it necessarily "better" than any other style. But when well used, as it is by Cunningham, it is rock solid. And his finest poems and epigrams will hold their freshness and vivacity as long as verse in English is read and written.

Cunningham and the Epigram

It is natural that Cunningham developed an interest in the epigram: not only is it a medium suited to a "short-breathed" person, it is also, along with satire and verse epistle, one of the poetic genres historically associated with the plain style. According to Cicero *(Orator,* 89–90), the plain stylist "will use wit and humor *(sale et facetiis).* . . . For my part, I judge this to be the pattern of the plain orator —plain but great and truly Attic; since whatever is witty and wholesome in speech *(salsum aut salubre in oratione)* is peculiar to the Athenian orators." No other poetic genre encourages pointedness and wit more than the epigram does; it is a form singularly useful to someone drawn to the plain style.

Yet if the plain style is misunderstood today, so is the epigram. Many treat it merely as a species of light verse, associating it narrowly with humor, especially humor of the ribald variety. Admittedly, epigrams are often humorous, and not a few are ribald. But through the ages the form has been put to all sorts of uses, serious as well as light. *Epigramma* means "inscription" in Greek, and in classical times many epigrams were literally inscribed on public monuments and commemorated or addressed the weightiest of civic issues and events. Simonides' famous two-liner on the defenders at Thermopylae is a case in point. Similarly, if we examine the classification of the books of the *Palatine Anthology*—that huge

compendium of Greek epigrams that covers the period from the seventh cen-
tury B.C. up to the tenth century A.D.—we will be struck by the breadth of top-
ics on which epigrammatists have written. The categories include "Christian
Epigrams," "Amatory Epigrams," "Sepulchral Epigrams," "Hortatory and Ad-
monitory Epigrams," "Satirical and Convivial Epigrams," and "Arithmetical
Problems and Riddles." Hence if we associate the epigram with "wit," we
should think of that quality in terms of dexterous compactness rather than in
terms of any particular tone or subject.

This point is illustrated by Cunningham's epigrams, which range from low
naughtiness,

> Lip was a man who used his head.
> He used it when he went to bed
> With his friend's wife, and with his friend,
> With either sex at either end.

to agile but serious satire,

> This Humanist whom no beliefs constrained
> Grew so broad-minded he was scatter-brained.

to bitter self-commentary,

> Hang up your weaponed wit
> Who were destroyed by it.
> If silence fails, then grace
> Your speech with commonplace,
> And studiously amaze
> Your audience with his phrase.
> He will commend your wit
> When you abandon it.

to telling philosophical analysis,

> Illusion and delusion are that real
> We segregate from real reality;
> But cause and consequence locate the real:
> What is not is also reality.

to somber reflection on the human condition:

> Life flows to death as rivers to the sea,
> And life is fresh and death is salt to me.

Indeed, in one poem, Cunningham takes as his subject this tonal and thematic range, saying: "I like the trivial, vulgar and exalted."

Given the range and number of his first-rate epigrams, Cunningham has, among English epigrammatists, only three peers: Ben Jonson, Robert Herrick, and Walter Savage Landor. And while he does not write the extended elegiac epigram that we find in Jonson and Herrick, Cunningham combines something of Jonson's saturnine intellectuality with the grace of Herrick or Landor.

Though most at ease with the plain style and the epigram, Cunningham does not confine himself to that mode and that form. He writes excellent poems early (e.g., "The Phoenix") and late (e.g., "Montana Fifty Years Ago") in manners with which he is not customarily identified. Also, Cunningham once stated that, as a young poet, he was much impressed by the verse of Swift, Landor, and Robinson.[20] Their influence dovetails with the other stylistic and generic preferences mentioned here. Swift, Landor, and Robinson are all to some degree plain stylists. Landor is an epigrammatist and Swift a satirist; Robinson is additionally significant in that he exhibits, in his analyses of human passions and relationships, something of the same compassionate fatalism that one finds in Cunningham.

The Text of This Book

A few words must be said about this edition of Cunningham's poems. Generally, editors follow the last text that the author saw through the press. However, Cunningham's last text, *The Collected Poems and Epigrams* of 1971, is problematical. Perhaps to distinguish it from his earlier collected poems, *The Exclusions of a Rhyme*, Cunningham in the 1971 volume dispensed with the arrangements of his original individual books and chapbooks. Instead, he separated the poems from the epigrams and ordered both chronologically. The poems appeared in sections headed with Roman numerals and inclusive dates—"I (1931–1934)," "II (1935–1941)," and so on—and the epigrams were merged into a one-hundred-item sequence called *A Century of Epigrams*.

This disposition of material produced several unfortunate consequences. First, it blunted one's sense of the variety of Cunningham's work. Mixed together as they were in his individual books, the poems and the epigrams nicely complemented one another. This is especially true of *The Helmsman,* in which the epigrams provided a leavening influence among the denser, more difficult poems. By the same token, the epigrams were diminished by their segregation. While their thematic range is impressive, Cunningham's epigrams are not as various in length or in meter as Jonson's or Herrick's are in English or as Catullus's or Martial's are in Latin. Ninety-three of the *Century of Epigrams* are from two to six lines long; seventy-nine are in iambic pentameter. As striking as the epigrams are individually, in congregation they may make one feel as one does reading a substantial group of Emily Dickinson's poems: after a point, the formal sameness dulls one's appreciation. If it be objected that having all the epigrams in one place enables one to admire Cunningham's mastery of the genre, it might be answered that this mastery is no less evident, without the hint of monotony, in the "Journal" of forty-three epigrams that concludes *The Judge Is Fury.*

A final reason to maintain the integrity of the original books is that they are interesting in and of themselves. As has been noted, *The Helmsman* is more than a gathering of discrete poems; it also records a search for personal and artistic fulfillment. And *The Judge Is Fury,* if lacking the narrative aspect of *The Helmsman,* is remarkable and shows Cunningham at the top of the game.

I have used, therefore, as the basis for this edition Cunningham's *Exclusions of a Rhyme,* which presents the individual collections as such. I have also included *To What Strangers, What Welcome* (1964) and most of the material that Cunningham subsequently published in *Some Salt* (1967) and *Let Thy Words Be Few* (1988), as well as most of the material that appeared for the first time in the *The Collected Poems and Epigrams* (1971). I have dropped certain of the later epigrams that seem below Cunningham's usual standards. As regards the translations, I have placed these in a separate section and have arranged them chronologically according to author (the earliest being Sappho, the latest George Buchanan). This is the procedure Cunningham followed both in *The Exclusions of a Rhyme* and in *The Collected Poems and Epigrams.* If I have not followed the general organization of the 1971 *Collected Poems and Epigrams,* I have given, for the individual poems, the last version that Cunningham published.

My editorial choices have been guided by a desire to make Cunningham's work available in the most engaging manner possible. If I have at points acted more according to my feelings as a reader and poet than according to the principles of a professional editor, I have done so because I believe that this is at present the approach that will best serve Cunningham. At some future date, there will be occasion for a variorum edition containing everything that he ever published or otherwise preserved. The editor of that volume will have the chance to examine and criticize the judgments that have determined this one.

Cunningham's Importance

Because Cunningham's style and interests never corresponded to the fashions of his time—and because his work is not well known today—I should like to close this introduction by stating why people who care about poems would enjoy and benefit from reading his.

First and foremost, Cunningham is a moving writer. He is, among other things, a fine love poet, whether writing about the light or the dark side of that emotion. And with his sensitivity to otherness, he well communicates a vivid and respectful appreciation of the precariousness of life. Further, for all of his own intelligence, he writes incisively of the limits of our understanding and of the value of acknowledging those limits.

Cunningham is as well a model of stylistic purity. He is simultaneously lucid and lively. More specifically, Cunningham has in abundance that key technical facility for writing traditional verse. He can coordinate, naturally and flexibly, good grammar with meter, stanza, and rhyme. And he deserves the study of poets and critics for this, if for no other, quality.

There is another reason that Cunningham is a particularly instructive figure for poets and students of poetry. He writes with a knowledge of the rhetorical tradition and employs it fruitfully. In the last two hundred and fifty years, poetry and rhetoric have largely parted company, to the detriment of both. It would be risible to suggest that a new golden age of verse would ensue if only contemporary writers and readers would rush down to the library and check out Cicero and Quintilian. But we seem to have lost the ability reasonably to discuss style, and we seem unable reasonably to coordinate thought and feeling and form and content. In his poems and prose alike, Cunningham provides a model—not the only model, but a good one—of an intelligent and tactful appreciation and use of neglected but still valuable elements of our literary past.

On a related note, Cunningham is important for having restored the epigram to the flexibility and seriousness that it had in antiquity and in Jonson. And if the epigram has recently enjoyed a revival—a revival manifested in the epigrammatic work of such poets as R. L. Barth, Wendy Cope, Dick Davis, Thom Gunn, X. J. Kennedy, Brad Leithauser, John Frederick Nims, Helen Pinkerton, Vikram Seth, and Richard Wilbur—this is chiefly due to Cunningham's influence.

Cunningham is, moreover, entertaining in a way that few other poets are. He can be laugh-out-loud funny or thought-provokingly clever on topics involving the history of ideas or Cantor's paradoxes about infinity. Nor need one dig and sift to find the gems among Cunningham's poems. He never indulged in junk verse. Almost all of his work is arresting in one way or another.

Cunningham is, further, an excellent satirical poet. We have not in the United States been friendly to satirical verse. We tend, regardless of our political or social persuasions, to be certain of the virtue of our views. And we are likely to condemn, as "ungenerous," "cynical," or "sour," anybody who exposes and makes light of our moral self-deceptions and intellectual inconsistencies. Yet for our individual and collective health, we should probably thank the Muses when they send us a satirist rather than returning him or her to Parnassus in favor of another namby-pamby singer who will reinforce the bromides of the hour.

Lastly, Cunningham is an American original. He was a poor Irish-Catholic kid from Montana who nevertheless received a rigorous education from the Jesuits and then became a poet while wandering the West during the Depression. These days, many talk about reexamining the canon and figures who have been wrongly marginalized. Mostly, discussion concerns issues of gender, race, and sexuality. While such issues are important, it might be worth reassessing authors and texts in light of aesthetic values, too. What Cunningham does, he does as well as anyone, and he merits the most serious attention of those interested in recovering unjustly neglected writers.

In his "Terse Elegy for J.V. Cunningham," X. J. Kennedy says of Cunningham that he

> . . . penned with patient skill and lore immense,
> Prodigious mind, keen ear, rare common sense,
> Only those words he could crush down no more
> Like matter pressured to a dwarf star's core.

And Kennedy adds:

> May one day eyes unborn wake to esteem
> His steady, baleful, solitary gleam.[21]

May living eyes find in this collection delight and profit, whether they are reading Cunningham's work for the first time or are reencountering it as a prized and reliable old friend.

Notes to the Introduction

1. J.V. Cunningham, *The Collected Essays of J. V. Cunningham* (Chicago: Swallow, 1976), 353. This work will hereafter be referred to as *CE*.

2. Timothy Steele, "An Interview with J. V. Cunningham," *The Iowa Review* 15 (Fall 1985), 6.

3. J. V. Cunningham, "Commencement Address, Lawrence University, 11 June 1978," *Folio* 17 (Spring 1980), 13–14.

4. Steele, "An Interview with J. V. Cunningham," 6.

5. Ibid., 11.

6. Ibid., 10.

7. The title of Cunningham's doctoral dissertation is "Tragic Effect and Tragic Process in Some Plays of Shakespeare, and Their Background in the Literary and Ethical Theory of Classical Antiquity and the Middle Ages." Cunningham subsequently cut down and rearranged the dissertation and published it in 1951 as *Woe or Wonder: The Emotional Effect of Shakespearean Tragedy.*

8. Steele, "An Interview with J. V. Cunningham," 11. Of his early relations with Winters, Cunningham said: "[O]f course, he was a dominant personality, and so, in my early days, was I; and I would imagine that we got along well for eight or ten days. Of course, I had been on the road, . . . and I was not really in good condition, psychically." Cunningham added of Janet Winters: "But I must say that Mrs. Winters, Janet Lewis, was not merely kind but human, and made perhaps all the difference."

9. J. V. Cunningham, Notes on Yvor Winters, *Collected Poems* (Denver, 1952); unpublished notes (Charlottesville, 1953), 2.

10. Yvor Winters, *Forms of Discovery* (Denver: Swallow, 1967), 300, 303.

11. Charles Gullans, *A Bibliography of the Published Works of J. V. Cunningham 1931–1988,* revised and enlarged (Florence, Ky.: Robert L. Barth, 1988), 40–44.

12. Horace, *Satires, Epistles and Ars Poetica,* ed. and trans. H. Rushton Fairclough (Loeb Classical Library [LCL], Cambridge: Harvard University Press, 1926). My translation.

13. Steele, "An Interview with J. V. Cunningham," 15.

14. The title page of *Let Thy Words Be Few* is dated 1986. But Gullans, whose Symposium Press issued the collection, notes in his *Bibliography*: "The book was in fact published on January 11, 1988."

15. Cf. Paul Oskar Kristeller on the theoretical schools that have dominated academic discussion of the humanities in recent decades: "The proponents of these approaches believe that they enrich history by imposing some present ideas on the past, but in fact they impoverish the present and the future by foregoing the chance of enriching modern readers with the additional or alternative ideas and insights that the literature of the past, much of it neglected or forgotten, can offer them" (*Renaissance Thought and the Arts,* expanded edition [Princeton: Princeton University Press, 1990], ix).

16. Richard Wilbur, *New and Collected Poems* (San Diego: Harcourt Brace, 1988), 130.

17. Illuminating discussions of Scotus and haecceity may be found in Frederick Copleston, *A History of Philosophy,* vol. 2, *Medieval Philosophy,* part 2 (Garden City, N.Y.: Doubleday, 1962), 223–40, and in the extended entry for "Duns Scotus" in William L. Reese, *Dictionary of Philosophy and Religion* (Atlantic Highlands, N.J.: Humanities Press, 1980). Winters notes *(Forms of Discovery,* 300) that Cunningham's view of haecceity recalls the plight of Valéry's serpent, though Winters does not discuss the philosophical background of the concept or speculate about the reasons that Cunningham may have interpreted the concept as he does.

18. For the ancient works mentioned in this section of the introduction, I have consulted the following editions: Demetrius, *On Style,* ed. and trans. by W. Rhys Roberts (LCL, Cambridge: Harvard University Press, 1927); Dionysius of Halicarnassus, *Critical Essays,* ed. and trans. by Stephen Usher (LCL, Cambridge: Harvard University Press, 1974); Cicero, *Orator,* ed. and trans. by H. M. Hubbell (LCL, Cambridge: Harvard University Press, 1971); Quintilian, *Institutio Oratoria,* ed. and trans. by H. E. Butler, 4 vols. (LCL, Cambridge: Harvard University Press, 1920–22); Plutarch, *Lives,* vol. 9, ed. and trans. by Bernadotte Perrin (LCL, Cambridge: Harvard University Press, 1920); and Plato, *Euthyphro, Apology, Crito, Phaedo, Phaedrus,* ed. and trans. by Harold North Fowler (LCL, Cambridge: Harvard University Press, 1914). Two fine works on the plain style in general are George Converse Fiske, "The Plain Style in the Scipionic Circle," *University of Wisconsin Studies in Language and Literature* 3 (1919), 62–105, and Wesley Trimpi, *Ben Jonson's Poems: A Study of the Plain Style* (Stanford: Stanford University Press, 1962). J. J. Pollitt, *The Ancient View of Greek Art* (New Haven: Yale University Press, 1974) has excellent discussions of the meanings and applications, in connection with the visual arts, of such terms as *leptos* and *subtilis.*

19. Socrates, with his insistence on speaking the truth and in his distrust of rhetorical embellishment, was regarded by later ancient writers, especially of the Stoic school, as an originator of the plain style (see Fiske, 86ff.); and Socrates' trial might be seen as another illustration of the advantages and disadvantages of plain style. Socrates tells the court he is not going to appeal to their emotions, but will instead cleave to facts and logic. He will try to instruct the jurors—instruction being one of the functions of the plain style—rather than play upon their sympathies. As he says (*Apology,* 34B–C, 35C), "Perhaps some one among you may be offended when he remembers his own conduct, if he, even in a case of less importance than this, begged and besought the judges with many tears, and brought forward his children to arouse compassion. . . . I [however] think it is not right to implore the judge or to get acquitted by begging; we ought to inform [*didaskein*—'teach'] and convince [*peithein*—'persuade by fair means']." (For relevant discussion of this last term, see the entry for *peithō* in Henry George Liddell and Robert Scott, *A Greek-English Lexicon,* 8th ed. [Oxford: Oxford University Press, 1897]). Socrates, in other words, is a kind of clearer-sighted Brutus. He knows his style does not suit the occasion. Yet believing in its virtue, he sticks with it, preferring honorable defeat to shameful triumph.

20. Steele, "An Interview with J. V. Cunningham," 14.

21. X. J. Kennedy, *Dark Horses* (Baltimore: Johns Hopkins University Press, 1992), 26.

THE HELMSMAN

1942

Of thirty years ten years I gave to rhyme
That that time should not pass: so passes time.

Lector Aere Perennior

Poets survive in fame.
But how can substance trade
The body for a name
Wherewith no soul's arrayed?

No form inspires the clay
Now breathless of what was
Save the imputed sway
Of some Pythagoras,

Some man so deftly mad
His metamorphosed shade,
Leaving the flesh it had,
Breathes on the words they made.

The Wandering Scholar's Prayer
to St. Catherine of Egypt

Past ruined cities down the grass,
Past wayside smokers in the shade,
Clicking their heels the fruit cars pass
Old stations where the night is stayed.

Curved on the racking wheel's retreat,
Sweet Catherine, rise from time to come,

Number in pain the fruit car fleet,
And throw confusion in the sum!

The vagrants smoke in solitude,
Sick of the spittle without cough;
Not unabsolved do they grow rude,
Dying with Swift in idiot froth.

From revery, sweet saint, forfend
Those ravelled faces of the park!
When questing cars at twilight's end
Cozen the eyes with chilling dark,

Save them from memory of the light,
The circuit of the orient sun
Wheeling loud silence through the night
Like headlamps where the twin rails run.

The Dogdays

> hic in reducta valle Caniculae
> vitabis aestus . . .

The morning changes in the sun
As though the hush were insecure,
And love, so perilously begun,
Could never in the noon endure,

The noon of unachieved intent,
Grown hazy with unshadowed light,
Where changing is subservient
To hope no longer, nor delight.

Nothing alive will stir for hours,
Dispassion will leave love unsaid,

While through the window masked with flowers
A lone wasp staggers from the dead.

Watch now, bereft of coming days,
The wasp in the darkened chamber fly,
Whirring ever in an airy maze,
Lost in the light he entered by.

Elegy for a Cricket

at vobis male sit, malae tenebrae
Orci, quae omnia bella devoratis!

Fifteen nights I have lain awake and called you
But you walk ever on and give no answer:
Therefore, damned by my sole, go down to hellfire.
Spirit luminous and footstep uncertain,
You will pace off forever the halls of great Dis.
You there, caught in the whirling throng of lovers,
If you find in that fire her whom I loved once,
Say to her that I gave you few but true words.
Say to her that your dream as her dream held me,
Alone, waking, until your friend, the cock, slept.
Say to her, if she ask what shoe you wear now,
That I gave you my last, I have none other.

All Choice Is Error

This dry and lusty wind has stirred all night
The tossing forest of one sleepless tree,
And I in waking vision walked with her
Whose hair hums to the motion of the forest
And in the orbit of whose eyelids' fall
The clouds drift slowly from the starry wharves.
I knew her body well but could not speak,
For comprehension is a kind of silence,
The last harmonic of all sound. Europa,
Iö, and Danaë: their names are love
Incarnate in the chronicles of love.
I trace their sad initials which thy bark,
Gaunt tree, may line with age but not efface,
And carve her name with mine there. The tree is gnarled
And puckered as a child that looks away
And fumbles at the breast—prodigious infant
Still sucking at the haggard teats of time,
Radical change, the root of human woe!

All choice is error, the tragical mistake,
And you are mine because I name you mine.
Kiss, then, in pledge of the imponderables
That tilt the balance of eternity
A leaf's weight up and down. Though we must part
While each dawn darkens on the fortunate wheel,
The moon will not soften our names cut here
Till every sheltering bird has fled the nest.
They know the wind brings rain, and rain and wind
Will smooth the outlines of our lettering
To the simplicity of epitaph.

Obsequies for a Poetess

The candles gutter in her quiet room,
And retrospect, returning through the sad
Degrees of dusk that had o'ershadowed pain,
Finds her Lethean source, the unmemoried stream
Of cold sensation. There, vain Sibylls clothed
In solemn ash, their hair dishevelled, weep
The close of centuries where time like stanzas
Stands in division, disposed, and none
Dare chant antiphonal to that strain. Pale Aubrey
Finds there his faint and final rest; there Dowson
Pillows his fond head on each breast. For them
And their compeers, our blind and exiled ghosts
Which nightly gull us with oblivion,
Weave we this garland of deciduous bloom
With subtle thorn. Their verse, sepulchral, breathes
A careless scent of flowers in late July,
Too brief for pleasure, though its pleasure lie
In skilled inconscience of its brevity.

The Symposium

Over the heady wine,
Well-watered with good sense,
Come sing the simple line
And charm confusion hence.

The fathers on the shelves
Surely approve our toasts,
Surely are here themselves,
Warm, amiable ghosts,

Glad to escape the new
Regenerate elect
Who take the social view
And zealously reject

The classic indignation,
The sullen clarity
Of passions in their station,
Moved by propriety.

The Beacon

Men give their hearts away;
Whether for good or ill
    They cannot say
Who shape the object in their will.

The will in pure delight
Conceives itself. I praise
    Far lamps at night,
Cold landmarks for reflection's gaze.

Distant they still remain,
Oh, unassailed, apart!
    May time attain
The promise ere death seals the heart!

Fancy

Keep the quick eyes hid in the mind!
Unleash them when the game is spied!
Free-reined fancy will but make blind
Your carnal soul, flesh glorified.

But firm fancy, untimely stayed,
Fixed on the one shape, still rehearsed,
Becomes the idol that it made,
Possessed by pure matter, accursed.

The hot flesh and passionless mind
In fancy's house must still abide,
Each share the work, its share defined
By caution under custom's guide.

The Helmsman: An Ode

The voyage of the soul is simply
    Through age to wisdom;
        But wisdom, if it comes,
Comes like the ripening gleam of wheat,

Nourished by comfort, care, rain, sunlight,
    And briefly shining
        On windy and hot days,
Flashing like snakes underneath the haze.

But this, a memory of childhood,
    Of loves forgotten,

And they who gave are still,
Gone now, irrevocable, undone.

O Penury, steadied to your will,
   I tread my own path,
      Though Self-Respect, discreet,
Plucks at my arm as I pass down street,

Querulous and pert. They tell in story
   That for proud Ajax,
      Vaingloriously self-slain,
Teucer set forth from his friends and kin;

He on the western shore of parting
   Paused to address them:
      "Comrades who have with me
Countless misfortunes endured, O mine!

Brave friends, banish tonight dark sorrow;
   Set the white tables
      With garlands, lamps, with wine;
Drink and, tomorrow, untravelled seas!"

So sailed guileful Odysseus, so sailed
   Pious Aeneas,
      And cloudless skies brought sleep,
Stilling th' unmasterable, surging deep,

The helmsman stilled, his sea-craft guiding.
   O too confiding
      In star and wind and wave,
Naked you lie in an unknown grave.

Hymn in Adversity

Fickle mankind!
When force and change
Wildly derange
The casual mind
    On chance begotten,

Trust in the Lord,
For that is best.
As for the rest,
Though not ignored
    And not forgotten,

The heart not whole
Nor quite at ease,
Here finds some peace,
Some wealth of soul,
    Albeit ill-gotten.

A Moral Poem

Then leave old regret,
Ancestral remorse,
Which, though you forget,
Unseen keep their course;

Shaping what each says,
Weathered in his style,

They in his fond ways
Live on for a while.

But leave them at last
To find their own home.
Inured to the past,
Be what you become:

Nor ungrudgingly
The young hours dispense,
Nor live curiously,
Cheating providence.

Timor Dei

Most beautiful, most dear,
When I would use Thy light,
Beloved, omniscient Seer,
Thou didst abuse my sight;

Thou didst pervade my being
Like marsh air steeped in brine;
Thou didst invade my seeing
Till all I saw was Thine.

Today, from my own fence
I saw the grass fires rise,
And saw Thine old incense
Borne up in frosty sighs.

Most terrible, most rude,
I will not shed a tear
For lost beatitude,
But I still fear Thy fear.

Choice

Allegiance is assigned
Forever when the mind
Chooses and stamps the will.
Thus, I must love you still
Through good and ill.

But though we cannot part
We may retract the heart
And build such privacies
As self-regard agrees
Conduce to ease.

So manners will repair
The ravage of despair
Which generous love invites,
Preferring quiet nights
To vain delights.

Summer Idyll

There is a kind of privacy,
Immobile as the windless wheat,
Within whose dusty seignory
We ripen with maturing heat.

Dreamless repose, unvisioned rest,
Gold harvest that we will not reap,
Perfect the sleeper on your breast!
And if he wake not? He will sleep.

For My Contemporaries

How time reverses
The proud in heart!
I now make verses
Who aimed at art.

But I sleep well.
Ambitious boys
Whose big lines swell
With spiritual noise,

Despise me not,
And be not queasy
To praise somewhat:
Verse is not easy.

But rage who will.
Time that procured me
Good sense and skill
Of madness cured me.

EPIGRAMS

[1] *An Epitaph for Anyone*

An old dissembler who lived out his lie
Lies here as if he did not fear to die.

[2] *The Scarecrow*

His speech is spare,
An orchard scare
With battered hat;
Face rude and flat,
Whose painted eye
Jove's flashing doom
From broken sky
Can scarce illume:
The Thunderer
May strike his ear,
And no reply.

[3] *With a Detective Story*

Old friend, you'll know by this how scholars live:
The scholar is a mere conservative,
A man whose being is in what is not,
The proud tradition and the poisoned plot.
He is bewildered in the things that were,
He thrives on sherry and the murderer,
And with his bottle on a rainy night
By Aristotle's saws brings crimes to light.
    So with this murderer may you make merry
    And we'll redeem him with a glass of sherry.

Jove courted Danaë with golden love,
But you're not Danaë, and I'm not Jove.

[5] The Lover's Ghost Returns to the Underworld

Farewell, false love! Dawn and Lethean doom
Recall me. Where I go you too must come.
Others possess you here: there, mine alone,
You will sleep with me, grinding bone to bone.

[6]

Homer was poor. His scholars live at ease,
Making as many Homers as you please,
And every Homer furnishes a book.
Though guests be parasitic on the cook
The moral is: *It is the guest who dines.*
I'll write a book to prove I wrote these lines.

[7]

Time heals not: it extends a sorrow's scope
As goldsmiths gold, which we may wear like hope.

August Hail

In late summer the wild geese
In the white draws are flying.
The grain beards in the blue peace.
The weeds are drying.

The hushed sky breeds hail.
Who shall revenge unreason?
Wheat headless in the white flail
Denies the season.

Montana Pastoral

I am no shepherd of a child's surmises.
I have seen fear where the coiled serpent rises,

Thirst where the grasses burn in early May
And thistle, mustard, and the wild oat stay.

There is dust in this air. I saw in the heat
Grasshoppers busy in the threshing wheat.

So to this hour. Through the warm dusk I drove
To blizzards sifting on the hissing stove,

And found no images of pastoral will,
But fear, thirst, hunger, and this huddled chill.

This Tower of Sun

There is no stillness in this wood.
The quiet of this clearing
Is the denial of my hearing
The sounds I should.

There is no vision in this glade.
This tower of sun revealing
The timbered scaffoldage is stealing
Essence from shade.

Only my love is love's ideal.
The love I could discover
In these recesses knows no lover,
Is the unreal,

The undefined, unanalysed,
Unabsolute many;
It is antithesis of any,
In none comprised.

Autumn

Gather the heart! The leaves
Fall in the red day. Grieves
No man more than the season.
Indifference is my guide.

Heart mellow and hope whirling
In a wild autumn hurling
Is time, and not time's treason.
And fatigue is my bride.

But say what moralist
Shall in himself subsist?
The tried. And you, occasion,
Far in my heart shall hide.

I have watched trains recede
Into that distance. Heed,
O heed not their persuasion
Who in no lands abide!

Reason and Nature

This pool in a pure frame,
This mirror of the vision of my name,
    Is a fiction
On the unrippled surface of reflection.

I see a willowed pool
Where the flies skim. Its angles have no rule.
    In no facet
Is the full vision imaged or implicit.

I've heard, in such a place
Narcissus sought the vision of his face.
    If the water
Concealed it, could he, drowning, see it better?

I know both what I see
And what I think, to alter and to be,
    And the vision
Of this informs that vision of confusion.

L'Esprit de Géométrie et L'Esprit de Finesse

In anima hominis dominatur violentia rationis.

St. Bonaventure

Qui ne sait que la vue de chats, de rats, l'écrasement d'un charbon, etc., emportent la raison hors des gonds?

Pascal

Yes, we are all
By sense or thought
Distraught.
The violence of reason rules
The subtle Schools;
A falling ember has unhinged Pascal.

I know such men
Of wild perceptions.
Conceptions
Cold as the serpent and as wise
Have held my eyes:
Their fierce impersonal forms have moved my pen.

Bookplate

Read me, ere age
Blot out this line.
Then will thy page,
Secure and whole
Though flaked like mine,
Pray for my soul,
And mine for thine.

THE JUDGE IS FURY

1947

These the assizes: here the charge, denial,
Proof and disproof: the poem is the trial.
Experience is defendant, and the jury
Peers of tradition, and the judge is fury.

The Phoenix

More than the ash stays you from nothingness!
Nor here nor there is a consuming pyre!
Your essence is in infinite regress
That burns with varying consistent fire,
Mythical bird that bears in burying!

I have not found you in exhausted breath
That carves its image on the Northern air,
I have not found you on the glass of death
Though I am told that I shall find you there,
Imperturbable in the final cold,

There where the North wind shapes white cenotaphs,
There where snowdrifts cover the fathers' mound,
Unmarked but for these wintry epitaphs,
Still are you singing there without sound,
Your mute voice on the crystal embers flinging.

In Innocence

In innocence I said,
"Affection is secure.
It is not forced or led."
No longer sure

Of the least certainty
I have erased the mind,
As mendicants who see
Mimic the blind.

Noon

I have heard the self's stir,
Anonymous
And low, as on the stair
At time of Angelus

The worshippers repeat
An exorcism,
The angled clock's repute
Conjured with chrism.

Distinctions at Dusk

Closed in a final rain
Clouds are complete,
Vows of shadowful light
Are vain,
And every hour is late.

Pride is a sky ingrown,
Selfishly fond,
By the edged sun nor found
Nor known,
But in the dusk defined.

Ripeness Is All

Let us not live with Lear,
Not ever at extremes
Of ecstasy and fear,
Joy in what only seems,
Rage in the madman's hut
Or on the thunderous hill,
Crying *To kill, to kill!*
Nor in a blind desire
To sire we know not what
Ravish the eternal Will.

The Chase

The rabbit crossed and dodged and turned;
I'd swear she neither saw nor heard
But ran for pleasure, unconcerned,
Erratic as a garden bird,

Timid and shy, but not afraid.
Say that her life was in the chase,
Yet it was nothing that God made
But wild blood glorying in a race

Through the cornfields of the lower Kaw.
My horse was tired before she fell.
Love does not work by natural law,
But as it is it's just as well,

For when the dogs retreated, fought,
And circled the embarrassed doe,
The doe moved only to be caught,
Self-pleased to be encircled so.

And I sat still, gun at my side.
Esteem and wonder stayed desire.
The kill is down. Time will abide.
Time to remember and inquire.

Coffee

When I awoke with cold
And looked for you, my dear,
And the dusk inward rolled,
Not light or dark, but drear,

Unabsolute, unshaped,
That no glass can oppose,
I fled not to escape
Myself, but to transpose.

I have so often fled
Wherever I could drink
Dark coffee and there read
More than a man would think

That I say I waste time
For contemplation's sake:
In an uncumbered clime
Minute inductions wake,

Insight flows in my pen.
I know nor fear nor haste.
Time is my own again.
I waste it for the waste.

To a Friend, on Her Examination for the Doctorate in English

After these years of lectures heard,
Of papers read, of hopes deferred,
Of days spent in the dark stacks
In learning the impervious facts
So well you can dispense with them,
Now that the final day has come
When you shall answer name and date
Where fool and scholar judge your fate
What have you gained?
                              A learnèd grace
And lines of knowledge on the face,
A spirit weary but composed
By true perceptions well-disposed,
A soft voice and historic phrase
Sounding the speech of Tudor days,
What ignorance cannot assail
Or daily novelty amaze,
Knowledge enforced by firm detail.

What revels will these trials entail,
What gentle wine confuse your head
While gossip lingers on the dead
Till all the questions wash away,
For you have learned, not what to say,
But how the saying must be said.

Passion

Passion is never fact
And never in a kiss,
For it is pure unact,
All other than the this.

It is love's negative,
Love's furious potency,
Distinct from which we live
In the affirmed to be.

And as love's passive form
Is not this form I see
But all the loves that swarm
In the unwilled to be,

So in this actual kiss,
Unfaithful, I am true:
I realize in this
All passion, act, and you.

The Metaphysical Amorist

You are the problem I propose,
My dear, the text my musings glose:
I call you for convenience love.
By definition you're a cause
Inferred by necessary laws—
You are so to the saints above.

But in this shadowy lower life
I sleep with a terrestrial wife
And earthy children I beget.
Love is a fiction I must use,
A privilege I can abuse,
And sometimes something I forget.

Now, in the heavenly other place
Love is in the eternal mind
The luminous form whose shade she is,
A ghost discarnate, thought defined.
She was so to my early bliss,
She is so while I comprehend
The forms my senses apprehend,
And in the end she will be so.

Her whom my hands embrace I kiss,
Her whom my mind infers I know.
The one exists in time and space
And as she was she will not be;
The other is in her own grace
And is *She is* eternally.

Plato! you shall not plague my life.
I married a terrestrial wife.
And Hume! she is not mere sensation
In sequence of observed relation.
She has two forms—ah, thank you, Duns!—,
I know her in both ways at once.
I knew her, yes, before I knew her,
And by both means I must construe her,
And none among you shall undo her.

Envoi

Hear me, whom I betrayed
While in this spell I stayed,
Anger, cathartic aid,
Hear and approve my song!

See from this sheltered cove
The symbol of my spell
Calm for adventure move,
Wild in repose of love,
Sea-going on a shell
In a moist dream. How long—
Time to which years are vain—
I on this coastal plain,
Rain and rank weed, raw air,
Served that fey despair,
Far from the lands I knew!

Winds of my country blew
Not with such motion—keen,
Stinging, and I as lean,
Savage, direct, and bitten,
Not pitying and unclean.

Anger, my ode is written.

Not for Charity

What is it to forgive?
It is not to forget,
To forfeit memory
    In which I live.
It is to be in debt
To those who injure me.

If then I shall forgive
And consciously resign
My claim in love's estate
        In which I live,
Know that the choice is mine
And is the same as hate.

Say then that I forgive.
I choose indignity
In which my passions burn
        While I shall live,
O not for Charity,
But for my old concern.

The Predestined Space

Simplicity assuages
With grace the damaged heart,
So would I in these pages
If will were art.

But the best engineer
Of metre, rhyme, and thought
Can only tool each gear
To what he sought

If chance with craft combines
In the predestined space
To lend his damaged lines
Redeeming grace.

Acknowledgement

Your book affords
The peace of art,
Within whose boards
The passive heart

Impassive sleeps,
And like pressed flowers,
Though scentless, keeps
The scented hours.

Ars Amoris

Speak to her heart.
That manic force
When wits depart
Forbids remorse.

Dream with her dreaming
Until her lust
Seems to her seeming
An act of trust.

Do without doing.
Love's wilful potion
Veils the ensuing,
And brief, commotion.

Haecceity

Evil is any this or this
Pursued beyond hypothesis.

It is the scribbling of affection
On the blank pages of perfection.

Evil is presentness bereaved
Of all the futures it conceived,

Wilful and realized restriction
Of the insatiate forms of fiction.

It is this poem, or this act.
It is this absolute of fact.

Convalescence

I found that consciousness itself betrays
Silence, the fever of my harried days.

In the last circle of infirmity
Where I almost attained simplicity—

So to recite as if it were not said,
So to renounce as if one lost instead—

My unabandoned soul withdrew abhorred.
I knew oblivion was its own reward,

But pride is life, and I had longed for death
Only in consciousness of indrawn breath.

To My Daimon

Self-knower, self-aware,
Accomplice in despair,

Silence and shade increase
In corridors of peace

Till in a chapeled prayer
Warm grace wells from despair—

But if my heart offend me,
Daimon, can you defend me?

Who know myself within
The sinner and the sin.

The Man of Feeling

The music of your feeling has its form,
And its symphonic solitude affirms
The resonance of self, remote and warm,
With private acmes at appointed terms.

So yours, so mine. And no one overhears.
O sealed composer of an endless past,
Rejoice that in that harmony of spheres
Pythagoras and Protagoras fuse at last!

The Solipsist

There is no moral treason;
Others are you. Your *hence*
Is personal consequence;
Desire is reason.

There is no moral strife.
None falls in the abysm
Who dwells there, solipsism
His way of life.

Agnosco Veteris Vestigia Flammae

I have been here. Dispersed in meditation,
I sense the traces of the old surmise—
Passion dense as fatigue, faithful as pain,
As joy foreboding. O my void, my being
In the suspended sources of experience,
Massive in promise, unhistorical
Being of unbeing, of all futures full,
Unrealized in none, how love betrays you,
Turns you to process and a fluid fact
Whose future specifies its past, whose past
Precedes it, and whose history is its being.

Distraction

I have distracted time.
In a full day your face
Has only its own place.
Tired from irrelevance
I sleep, and dream by chance,
Till passion can exact
No faith, and fails in act,
Till timelessness recedes
Beneath the apparent needs
Of a distracted time.

Meditation on Statistical Method

Plato, despair!
We prove by norms
How numbers bear
Empiric forms,

How random wrong
Will average right
If time be long
And error slight;

But in our hearts
Hyperbole
Curves and departs
To infinity.

Error is boundless.
Nor hope nor doubt,
Though both be groundless,
Will average out.

Meditation on a Memoir

Who knows his will?
Who knows what mood
His hours fulfil?
His griefs conclude?

Surf of illusion
Spins from the deep
And skilled delusion
Sustains his sleep.

When silence hears
In its delight
The tide of tears
In the salt night,

And stirs, and tenses,
Who knows what themes,
What lunar senses,
Compel his dreams?

To the Reader

Time will assuage.
Time's verses bury
Margin and page
In commentary,

For gloss demands
A gloss annexed
Till busy hands
Blot out the text,

And all's coherent.
Search in this gloss
No text inherent:
The text was loss.

The gain is gloss.

EPIGRAMS: A JOURNAL

[1]

Each that I loved is now my enemy
To whom I severally inscribe my journal,
Who was defrauded of my vanity,
Peeled like a grain of wheat to the white kernel.

[2]

I don't know what I am. I think I know
Much of the circumstance in which I flow.
But knowledge is not power; I am that flow
Of history and of percept which I know.

[3]

If I can't know myself it's something gained
To help my enemy to know his sin,
Especially since in him it's only feigned,
For the ideal exemplar lies within.

[4]

Give not yourself to apology.
Yourself know, and slyly surprise
Passion, rework it, and let be.
Who is as he is is most wise.

[5] *With a Book of Clavier Music*

Discursive sense, unthought, unclear,
Is in this music planned;
Error is not of nature here
But of the human hand.

[6]

My dear, though I have left no sigh
Carved on your stone, yet I still cherish
Your name, and your flesh will not die
Till I and my descendants perish.

[7]

All hastens to its end. If life and love
Seem slow it is their ends we're ignorant of.

[8]

If wisdom, as it seems it is,
Be the recovery of some bliss
From the conditions of disaster—
Terror the servant, man the master—
It does not follow we should seek
Crises to prove ourselves unweak.
Much of our lives, God knows, is error,
But who will trifle with unrest?
These fools who would solicit terror,
Obsessed with being unobsessed,
Professionals of experience
Who have disasters to withstand them

As if fear never had unmanned them,
Flaunt a presumptuous innocence.

I have preferred indifference.

[9]

Within this mindless vault
Lie Tristan and Isolt
Tranced in each other's beauties.
They had no other duties.

[10]

Grief restrains grief as dams torrential rain,
And time grows fertile with extended pain.

[11]

When I shall be without regret
And shall mortality forget,
When I shall die who lived for this,
I shall not miss the things I miss.
And you who notice where I lie
Ask not my name. It is not I.

[12]

I was concerned for you and keep that part
In these days, irrespective of the heart:
And not for friendship, not for love, but cast
In that role by the presence of the past.

[13] On the Cover of My First Book

This garish and red cover made me start.
I who amused myself with quietness
Am here discovered. In this flowery dress
I read the wild wallpaper of my heart.

[14]

What is this visage? in what fears arrayed?
This ghost I conjured though that ghost was laid?
The vision of a vision still unstayed
By my voice, still by its own fears dismayed!

[15]

Deep summer, and time pauses. Sorrow wastes
To a new sorrow. While time heals time hastes.

[16]

The dry soul rages. The unfeeling feel
With the dry vehemence of the unreal.
So I in the Idea of your arms, unwon,
Am as the real in the unreal undone.

[17]

Dear, if unsocial privacies obsess me,
If to my exaltations I be true,
If memories and images possess me,
Yes, if I love you, what is that to you?
My folly is no passion for collusion.
I cherish my illusions as illusion.

[18]

Deep sowing of our shame, rage of our need,
Gross shadow of Idea, impersonal seed,
Unclothed desire! the malice of your thrust
Is his to use who takes his love on trust.

[19]

In this child's game where you grow warm and warmer,
And new grand passions still exceed the former,
In what orgasm of high sentiment
Will you conclude and sleep at last content?

[20]

After some years Bohemian came to this,
This Maenad with hair down and gaping kiss
Wild on the barren edge of under fifty.
She would finance his art if he were thrifty.

[21]

Genius is born and made. This heel who mastered
By infinite pains his trade was born a bastard.

[22]

I showed some devils of a moral kind
To a good friend who had a Freudian mind.
Doctor, there was no need for therapy.
I should have had myself to comfort me.

[23]

Dark thoughts are my companions. I have wined
With lewdness and with crudeness, and I find
Love is my enemy, dispassionate hate
Is my redemption though it come too late,
Though I come to it with a broken head
In the cat-house of the dishevelled dead.

[24]

Action is memoir: you may read my story
Even in pure thought, scandal in allegory.

[25] Motto for a Sun Dial

I who by day am function of the light
Am constant and invariant by night.

[26] History of Ideas

God is love. Then by conversion
Love is God, and sex conversion.

[27] On the Calculus

From almost naught to almost all I flee,
And *almost* has almost confounded me,
Zero my limit, and infinity.

[28]

Soft found a way to damn me undefended:
I was forgiven who had not offended.

[29]

Kiss me goodbye, to whom I've only been
Cause for uncloistered virtue, not for sin.

[30]

This Humanist whom no beliefs constrained
Grew so broad-minded he was scatter-brained.

[31]

He weeps and sleeps with Dido, calls him cad
Who followed God, and finds real Didos bad.

[32]

This is my curse. Pompous, I pray
That you believe the things you say
And that you live them, day by day.

[33]

Silence is noisome, but the loud logician
Raises more problems by their definition.
Then let your discourse be a murmured charm
And so ambiguous none hears its harm.

[34]

How we desire desire! Joy of surcease
In joy's fulfilment is bewildered peace,
And harsh renewal. Life in fear of death
Will trivialize the void with hurrying breath,
With harsh indrawal. Nor love nor lust impels us.
Time's hunger to be realised compels us.

[35]

Hang up your weaponed wit
Who were destroyed by it.
If silence fails, then grace
Your speech with commonplace,
And studiously amaze
Your audience with his phrase.
He will commend your wit
When you abandon it.

[36]

The self is terrified, shade calls to shade,
Ghost destroys ghost whose ghost springs undismayed,
And fear regresses to infinity.
I know the spell in the mythology
Of this despair, I know love's charms affright
Psychotic goblins in the Gothic night,
I know your arms. Dear, in that incantation
Despair in joy attains its consummation.

[37]

The scholar of theology and science
Who falls in love must in good faith affiance
Love and his trades; must prove the commonplace
Of his divine research, *Love goes by grace,*
Never by merit; judge by divination
Supernal from infernal visitation;
And risk his faith. As scientist he tries
By the inductive leap, immense surmise,
To force the future to confirm his guess,
Though predisposed toward ill or good success,
Pledged to the issue. So he may discover
As scholar truth, sincerity as lover.

[38]

Dear, my familiar hand in love's own gesture
Gives irresponsive absence flesh and vesture.

[39]

> Death in this music dwells. I cease to be
> In this attentive, taut passivity.

[40] To a Student

> Fiction, but memoir. Here you know
> Motive and act who made them so.
> Life falls in scenes; its tragedies
> Close in contrived catastrophes.
> Much is evasion. Some years pass
> With *Some years later.* In this glass
> Reflection sees reflection's smile
> And self-engrossment is good style.
>
> Fiction is fiction: its one theme
> Is its allegiance to its scheme.
> Memoir is memoir: there your heart
> Awaits the judgment of your art.
> But memoir in fictitious guise
> Is telling truth by telling lies.

[41] A Is A: Monism Refuted

> This Monist who reduced the swarm
> Of being to a single form,
> Emptying the universe for fun,
> Required two A's to think them one.

[42] *With a Copy of Swift's Works*

Underneath this pretty cover
Lies Vanessa's, Stella's lover.
You that undertake this story
For his life nor death be sorry
Who the Absolute so loved
Motion to its zero moved,
Till, immobile in that chill,
Fury hardened in the will,
And the trivial, bestial flesh
In its jacket ceased to thresh,
And the soul none dare forgive
Quiet lay, and ceased to live.

[43]

In whose will is our peace? Thou happiness,
Thou ghostly promise, to thee I confess
Neither in thine nor love's nor in that form
Disquiet hints at have I yet been warm;
And if I rest not till I rest in thee
Cold as thy grace, whose hand shall comfort me?

DOCTOR DRINK

1950

[1] In the Thirtieth Year

In the thirtieth year of life
I took my heart to be my wife,

And as I turn in bed by night
I have my heart for my delight.

No other heart may mine estrange
For my heart changes as I change,

And it is bound, and I am free,
And with my death it dies with me.

[2] *Interview with Doctor Drink*

I have a fifth of therapy
In the house, and transference there.
Doctor, there's not much wrong with me,
Only a sick rattlesnake somewhere

In the house, if it be there at all,
But the lithe mouth is coiled. The shapes
Of door and window move. I call.
What is it that pulls down the drapes,

Disheveled and exposed? Your rye
Twists in my throat: intimacy
Is like hard liquor. Who but I
Coil there and squat, and pay your fee?

[3]

Lip was a man who used his head.
He used it when he went to bed
With his friend's wife, and with his friend,
With either sex at either end.

[4]

Reader, it's time reality was faced:
My verse is naughty but my life is chaste.

[5] *Epitaph for Someone or Other*

Naked I came, naked I leave the scene,
And naked was my pastime in between.

[6]

All in due time: love will emerge from hate,
And the due deference of truth from lies.
If not quite all things come to those who wait
They will not need them: in due time one dies.

[7]

Dear child whom I begot,
Forgive me if my page
Hymns not your helpless age,
For you are mine, and not:
Mine as sower and sown,
But in yourself your own.

[8]

Life flows to death as rivers to the sea,
And life is fresh and death is salt to me.

[9]

On a cold night I came through the cold rain
And false snow to the wind shrill on your pane
With no hope and no anger and no fear.
Who are you? and with whom do you sleep here?

TRIVIAL, VULGAR, AND EXALTED

Uncollected Poems and Epigrams

1959

[1] On *Doctor Drink*

A reader (did he buy it, borrow, beg,
Or read it in a bookstore on one leg?)
Dislikes my book; calls it, to my discredit,
A book you can't put down before you've read it.
Yet in this paucity, this drouth of phrases,
There are as many as in children phases:
The trivial, vulgar, and exalted jostle
Each other in a way to make the apostle
Of culture and right feeling shudder faintly.
It is a shudder that affects the saintly.
It is a shudder by which I am faulted.
I like the trivial, vulgar and exalted.

[2]

Here lies my wife. Eternal peace
Be to us both with her decease.

[3]

My name is Ebenezer Brown.
I carted all the trash of town
For sixty years. On the last day
I trust my Lord will cart me away.

[4]

I married in my youth a wife.
She was my own, my very first.
She gave the best years of her life.
I hope nobody gets the worst.

[5]

Here lies New Critic who would fox us
With his poetic paradoxes.
Though he lies here rigid and quiet,
If he could speak he would deny it.

[6]

You wonder why Drab sells her love for gold?
To have the means to buy it when she's old.

[7]

You ask me how Contempt who claims to sleep
With every woman that has ever been
Can still maintain that women are skin deep?
They never let him any deeper in.

[8]

With every wife he can, and you know why?
Bold goes to bed because really he's shy.
And why I publish it none knows but I:
I publish it because really I'm shy.

[9]

Bride loved old words, and found her pleasure marred
On the first night, her expectations jarred,
And thirty inches short of being a yard.

[10]

Career was feminine, resourceful, clever.
You'd never guess to see her she felt ever
By a male world oppressed. How much they weigh!
Even her hand disturbed her as she lay.

[11]

Your affair, my dear, need not be a mess.
See at the next table with what finesse,
With what witty tensions and what tense wit,
As intricate as courtship, the love-fated
Sir Gawain and the Fay at lunch commit
Faithful adultery unconsummated.

[12]

The Elders at their services begin
With paper offerings. They release from sin
The catechumens on the couches lying
In visions, testimonies, prophesying:
Not, "Are you saved?" they ask, but in informal
Insistent query, "Brother, are you normal?"

[13]

Arms and the man I sing, and sing for joy,
Who was last year all elbows and a boy.

[14]

The man who goes for Christian resignation
Will find his attitude his occupation.

[15]

Another novel, and the prostitute
And the initiate. I who have never known
The rite of artistry, or how to do it,
With meager manuscript sit here alone.

[16]

And now you're ready who while she was here
Hung like a flag in a calm. Friend, though you stand
Erect and eager, in your eye a tear,
I will not pity you, or lend a hand.

[17] *For a College Yearbook*

Somewhere on these bare rocks in some bare hall,
Perhaps unrecognized, wisdom and learning
Flash like a beacon on a sleeper's wall,
Ever distant and dark, ever returning.

[18]

Love, receive Lais' glass, the famous whore,
In whose reflection you appear no more.

[19]

I had gone broke, and got set to come back,
And lost, on a hot day and a fast track,
On a long shot at long odds, a black mare
By Hatred out of Envy by Despair.

[20]

Friend, on this scaffold Thomas More lies dead
Who would not cut the Body from the Head.

[21]

And what is love? Misunderstanding, pain,
Delusion, or retreat? It is in truth
Like an old brandy after a long rain,
Distinguished, and familiar, and aloof.

[22] Night-piece

Three matches in a folder, you and me.
I sit and smoke, and now there's only two,
And one, and none: a small finality
In a continuing world, a thing to do.
And you, fast at your book, whose fingers keep
Its single place as you sift down to sleep.

[23] New York: 5 March 1957

Lady, of anonymous flesh and face
In the half-light, in the rising embrace
Of my losses, in the dark dress and booth,
The stripper of the gawking of my youth,
Lady, I see not, care not, what you are.
I sit with beer and bourbon at this bar.

[24]

Good Fortune, when I hailed her recently,
Passed by me with the intimacy of shame
As one that in the dark had handled me
And could no longer recollect my name.

[25] Fear

Love, at what distance mine!
On whose disdain I dine
Unfed, unfamished, I
In your hid counsels lie.
I know your lover, fear.
His presence is austere
As winter air. He trembles
Though the taut face dissembles.
I know him: I am he.

[26] *The Aged Lover Discourses in the Flat Style*

There are, perhaps, whom passion gives a grace,
Who fuse and part as dancers on the stage,
But that is not for me, not at my age,
Not with my bony shoulders and fat face.
Yet in my clumsiness I found a place
And use for passion: with it I ignore
My gaucheries and yours, and feel no more
The awkwardness of the absurd embrace.

It is a pact men make, and seal in flesh,
To be so busy with their own desires
Their loves may be as busy with their own,
And not in union. Though the two enmesh
Like gears in motion, each with each conspires
To be at once together and alone.

[27] *Horoscope*

Out of one's birth
The magi chart his worth;
They mark the influence
Of hour and day, and weigh what thence

Will come to be.
I in their cold sky see
Neither Venus nor Mars;
It is the past that cast the stars

That guide me now.
In winter when the bough
Has lost its leaves, the storm
That piled them deep will keep them warm.

TO MY WIFE

Prefatory Poem to The Exclusions of a Rhyme

1960

To My Wife

And does the heart grow old? You know
In the indiscriminate green
Of summer or in earliest snow
A landscape is another scene,

Inchoate and anonymous,
And every rock and bush and drift
As our affections alter us
Will alter with the season's shift.

So love by love we come at last,
As through the exclusions of a rhyme,
Or the exactions of a past,
To the simplicity of time,

The antiquity of grace, where yet
We live in terror and delight
With love as quiet as regret
And love like anger in the night.

TO WHAT STRANGERS, WHAT WELCOME

A Sequence of Short Poems

1964

When we parted,
I told her I should see the King again,
And, having seen him, might go back again
To see her face once more. But I shall see
No more the lady Vivian. Let her love
What man she may, no other love than mine
Shall be an index of her memories.
I fear no man who may come after me,
And I see none. I see her, still in green,
Beside the fountain. I shall not go back. . . .
                    If I come not,
The lady Vivian will remember me,
And say: "I knew him when his heart was young,
Though I have lost him now. Time called him home,
And that was as it was; for much is lost
Between Broceliande and Camelot."

Edwin Arlington Robinson, *Merlin*, 7.425–42

[1]

I drive Westward. Tumble and loco weed
Persist. And in the vacancies of need,
The leisure of desire, whirlwinds a face
As luminous as love, lost as this place.

[2]

On either side of the white line
The emblems of a life appear
In turn: purpose like lodgepole pine
Competitive and thin, and fear

Agile as aspen in a storm.
And then the twilit harboring
In a small park. The room is warm.
And by the ache of travelling

Removed from all immediacy,
From all time, I as time grows late
Sense in disordered fantasy
The sound and smell of love and hate.

[3]

In a few days now when two memories meet
In that place of disease, waste, and desire
Where forms receptive, featureless, and vast
Find occupation, in that narrow dark,
That warm sweat of a carnal tenderness,
What figure in the pantheon of lust,
What demon is our god? What name subsumes
That act external to our sleeping selves?
Not pleasure—it is much too broad and narrow—,
Not sex, not for the moment love, but pride,
And not in prowess, but pride undefined,
Autonomous in its unthought demands,
A bit of vanity, but mostly pride.

[4]

You have here no otherness,
Unaddressed correspondent,
No gaunt clavicles, no hair
Of bushy intimacy.
You are not, and I write here
The name of no signature
To the unsaid—a letter
At midnight, a memorial
And occupation of time.

I'll not summon you, or feel
In the alert dream the give

And stay of flesh, the tactile
Conspiracy.
                    The snow falls
With its inveterate meaning,
And I follow the barbed wire
To trough, to barn, to the house,
To what strangers, what welcome
In the late blizzard of time.

On the highway cars flashing,
Occasional and random
As pain gone without symptom,
And fear drifts with the North wind.
We neither give nor receive:
The unfinishable drink
Left on the table, the sleep
Alcoholic and final
In the mute exile of time.

[5]

The soft lights, the companionship, the beers,
And night promises everything you lacked.
The short drive, the unmade bed, and night in tears
Hysteric in the elemental act.

[6]

It was in Vegas. Celibate and able
I left the silver dollars on the table
And tried the show. The black-out, baggy pants,
Of course, and then this answer to romance:
Her ass twitching as if it had the fits,
Her gold crotch grinding, her athletic tits,
One clock, the other counter clockwise twirling.
It was enough to stop a man from girling.

[7]

A traveller, the highway my guide,
And a little bastard of a dog
My friend. I have pin-ups for passion
As I go moseying about these scenes,
Myself improbable as yucca,
Illusory as the bright desert,
And finally here: the surf breaking,
Repetitive and varied as love
Enacted, and inevitably
The last rim of sunset on the sea.

[8]

The night is still. The unfailing surf
In passion and subsidence moves
As at a distance. The glass walls,
And redwood, are my utmost being.
And is there there in the last shadow,
There in the final privacies
Of unaccosted grace,—is there,
Gracing the tedium to death,
An intimation? Something much
Like love, like loneliness adrowse
In states more primitive than peace,
In the warm wonder of winter sun.

[9]

Innocent to innocent,
One asked, What is perfect love?
Not knowing it is not love,
Which is imperfect—some kind
Of love or other, some kind
Of interchange with wanting,
There when all else is wanting,
Something by which we make do.

So, impaired, uninnocent,
If I love you—as I do—
To the very perfection
Of perfect imperfection,
It's that I care more for you
Than for my feeling for you.

[10]

A half hour for coffee, and at night
An hour or so of unspoken speech,
Hemming a summer dress as the tide
Turns at the right time.
                  Must it be sin,
This consummation of who knows what?
This sharp cry at entrance, once, and twice?
This unfulfilled fulfilment?
                      Something
That happens because it must happen.
We live in the given. Consequence,
And lack of consequence, both fail us.
Good is what we can do with evil.

[11]

I drive Eastward. The ethics of return,
Like the night sound of coyotes on a hill
Heard in eroded canyons of concern,
Disposes what has happened, and what will.

[1 2]

Absence, my angel, presence at my side,
I know you as an article of faith
By desert, prairie, and this stonewalled road—
As much my own as is the thought of death.

[1 3]   *Nescit vox missa reverti . . .*

The once hooked ever after lives in lack,
And the once said never finds its way back.

[1 4]

I write only to say this,
In a syllabic dryness
As inglorious as I feel:
Sometime before drinking time
For the first time in some weeks
I heard of you, the casual
News of a new life, silence
Of unconfronted feeling
And maples in the slant sun
The gay color of decay.
Was it unforgivable,
My darling, that you loved me?

[15]

Identity, that spectator
Of what he calls himself, that net
And aggregate of energies
In transient combination—some
So marginal are they mine? Or is
There mine? I sit in the last warmth
Of a New England fall, and I?
A premise of identity
Where the lost hurries to be lost,
Both in its own best interests
And in the interests of life.

POEMS AND EPIGRAMS

1960–1970

[1]

I write you in my need. Please write
As simply, in terms black and white,
And do not fear hyperbole,
Uncompromising Flattery!
I can believe the best of me.

[2]

Illusion and delusion are that real
We segregate from real reality;
But cause and consequence locate the real:
What is not is also reality.

[3] *For a Woman with Child*

We are ourselves but carriers. Life
Incipient grows to separateness
And is its own meaning. Life is,
And not; there is no nothingness.

[4]

Old love is old resentment, novelty
Confined by expectation, ease and distance
Living together, with mute fantasy
A descant on the plainsong of persistence.

[5] Towards Tucson

In this attractive desolation,
A world's debris framed by a fence,
Drink is my only medication
And loneliness is my defence.

[6]

There is a ghost town of abandoned love
With tailings of used hope, leavings of risk,
Deserted cherishings masked with new life,
Where the once ugly is now picturesque.

[7] On a Line from Bodenham's "Belvedere"

"Experience is the mistress of old age:"
Kept at my cost, as old as I am, bitch
And parasite, I screw her in my rage
And would kill her, but which of us is which?

[8]

Who am I? I have pondered with my peers,
And unexisting existentially
For years I have gone sidelong through the years
And half faced and half assed reality.

[9]

I grow old, but I know that Science some
Few years from now will found millennium:
To be immortal, with an annual raise,
And practice continence on New Year's Days.

[10]

Young Sensitive one summer on the Cape
Met a Miss Splash. She led him to a rape
Through all the jagged colors of her mood.
It was like sleeping with an abstract nude.

[11] Love's Progress

Pal was her friend, her lover, and, dismissed,
Became at last her lay psychiatrist.

[12]

Mistress of scenes, good-by. Your maidenhead
Was fitter for the couch than for the bed.

[13] Modern Love

She has a husband, he a wife.
What a way to spend a life!
So whenever they are free
They synchronize adultery,
And neither one would dare to stop
Without a simultaneous plop.

[14]

Prue loved her man: to clean, to mend,
To have a child for his sake, fuss
Over him, and on demand
Sleep with him with averted face.

[15]

A faint smile of distraction, moist response
At the least touch, even her husband's. Can
Imaged adultery fulfil his wants
And still be sleeping with the other man?

[16]

An Oedipean Mom and Dad
Made Junior Freud feel pretty bad,
And when they died he was so vexed
He never after hetrosexed.

[17]

Some twenty years of marital agreement
Ended without crisis in disagreement.
What was the problem? Nothing of importance,
Nothing but money, sex, and self-importance.

[18]

A periphrastic insult, not a banal:
You are not a loud-mouthed and half-assed worm;
You are, sir, magni-oral, semi-anal,
A model for a prophylactic firm.

[19] Portrait

I am the other woman, so much other
It is no task to tell the one from tother.

[20] On a Letter

Unsigned, almost unsent, and all unsaid
Except the sending, which I take as read.

I, Too, Have Been to the Huntington

A railroad baron in the West
Built this nest,

With someone else's pick and shovel
Built this hovel,

And bought these statues semi-nude,
Semi-lewd,

Where ladies' bosoms are revealed,
And concealed,

And David equally with Venus
Has no penis.

The True Religion

The New Religion is the True,
A transformation overdue,
A thorough Freudly Reformation
Based like the old on a translation.
Their fear is our anxiety,
Our complex their humility.
The virtuous are now repressed,
The penitent are now depressed,
Even the elect are simply manic,
And chastity is pansy-panic.

In brief, the Convert is a Case.
He puts away all else to face
Reality with the paralysis
Of a seven year depth analysis.
He does not see but he is heard.
He is transferred and untransferred.
He has aggressions and no malice,
And phallic symbols and no phallus.

Monday Morning

The flattery has been infrequent
And somewhat grudging. There is junk mail
And no letter. The weather cloudy
With more snow. Fortuitous meeting,
The rustle of flirtation, the look—
Self-esteem sustained by any excuse,
By any misconstruction? No. No.
It is now a January world,
An after Christmas waiting. For what?
Not for this snow, this silence. There is
No resonance in the universe.
I must buy something extra today
And clutter up my house and my life.

Consolatio Nova

For Alan Swallow

To speak of death is to deny it, is
To give unpredicated substance phrase
And being. So the discontinuous,
The present instant absent finally
Without future or past, is yet in time
For we are time, monads of purposes
Beyond ourselves that are not purposes,
A causeless all of momentary somes.
And in such fiction we can think of death.

Think

Let us forget praise and blame,
Speak only of quietness
And survival. Mad toadstools
Grow in the dampness, englobed
Enormities, inherited
Treachery of all our pasts.
Forget. What was day is night.
In curtained sufficiency
Rest in the living silence,
Rest in arrogant sleep. Think
What houseflies have died in time.

Montana Fifty Years Ago

Gaunt kept house with her child for the old man,
Met at the train, dust-driven as the sink
She came to, the child white as the alkali.
To the West distant mountains, the Big Lake
To the Northeast. Dead trees and almost dead
In the front yard, the front door locked and nailed,
A handpump in the sink. Outside, a land
Of gophers, cottontails, and rattlesnakes,
In good years of alfalfa, oats, and wheat.
Root cellar, blacksmith shop, milk house, and barn,
Granary, corral. An old *World Almanac*
To thumb at night, the child coughing, the lamp smoked,
The chores done. So he came to her one night,
To the front room, now bedroom, and moved in.
Nothing was said, nothing was ever said.
And then the child died and she disappeared.
This was Montana fifty years ago.

LATE EPIGRAMS

1970–1982

[1]

Some good, some middling, and some bad
You'll find here. They are what I had.

After Martial, 1.16

[2]

Who lives by wisdom and to others gives
His wise advice, in that unwisely lives.

[3] *The Lights of Love*

The ladies in my life, serially sexed,
Unscrew one lover and screw in the next.

[4] *On Correggio's Leda*

Busied with private dreams, earthen, unspoken,
With drowsy weight, cool rest, and harvest sun,
Love threads your limbs, fulfilled, the dream unbroken:
So might I sleep on, you and I being one.

[5] Gnothi Seauton

The wise have known themselves. Some few
Recorded what it was they knew.
Then read those volumes on your shelves.
Who do you know who know your selves?

[6] Memoir

Now that he's famous fame will not elude me:
For 14.95 read how he screwed me.

[7] Original Sin

The trouble with my ex–
   Was mostly sex.
The trouble with my new
   Is the to-do.
The trouble with them all
   Was Adam's fall.

[8]

I have come home. Fortune and Hope, goodbye!
We've nothing left in common, you and I.

A. P., 9.49

[9] They

Of all the gods that were
Remains one deity:
Who do they think they are?
They can't do this to me.

[10] Cantor's Theorem: In an Infinite Class the Whole Is No Greater Than Some of Its Parts.

Euclid, alone, who looked in beauty's heart,
Assumed the whole was greater than the part;
But Cantor, with the infinite in control,
Proved that the part was equal to the whole.

[11]

If one takes trouble to explain
This signifies he is not sane;
His reasoning is but rationalizing.
And so it's not at all surprising
Your rationalizing is his reasoning.
He likes the soup who does the seasoning.

[12]

They said the Muses were but Nine, and then
    Sappho of Lesbos made them Ten.

Plato, *A.P.*, 9.506

[13] A Few Words, and Some His, In Memory of Clayton Stafford

All but the future is Antiquity.
Still from these broken shards of memory
May a few words for a few minutes stay
The necessary holocaust of time—
A few words, a casual legacy,
As of *love's essence, muteness,* heard by one
Who *had not known the silence of all speech.*

[14] 1 Corinthians 13: Commentary

Faith, Hope, and Love. Of these three is Love all?
It hears all, it believes all, endures all,
But hears, believes, endures only in Hope,
Of Faith begotten, from whom Love proceeds.

[15] Statistics

They both collected for the March of Dimes,
Just middle-aged and average. As they should,
They had coitus two-and-six-tenths times
A week. The six-tenth time was not so good.

[16] Jack and Jill

She said he was a man who cheated.
He said she didn't play the game.
She said an expletive deleted.
He said the undeleted same.
And so they ended their relation
With meaningful communication.

[17] Somnium Narrare, Vigilantis Est

Seneca, Epistola 53

Only the wide-awake can tell their dreams.
And you outside my window in the snow
Whose voices of the dark disturb my fear,
My fear, the formless spirit of my hopes,
Only your unknown tongue can tell it true.

[18] To Whom It May Concern

After so many decades of . . . of what?
I have a permanent sabbatical.
I pass my time on actuarial time,
Listen to music, and, going to bed,
Leave something in the bottom of the glass,
A little wastefulness to end the day.

TRANSLATIONS

1932–1981

SAPPHO

[LP 1]

Bright-throned, undying Aphrodite,
God's child, manipulator, hear me!
Destroy not with anguish and heartbreak,
      Lady, my spirit,

But come to me here if other times
You ever my voice in the distance
Have heard, and, leaving your father's house,
      Have come, your golden

Chariots yoked, your beautiful swift
Sparrows, dense-winged, spiraling above
The black earth, from th' heavenly aether
      Through the middle air,

And now here. You, of the Lucky Ones,
With a smile on your undying face,
Asked what now is the matter with me?
      Why now do I call?

What do I most wish for for myself
In my mad heart? "Who is it I must
Now win over for you? Who, Sappho,
      Is unfair to you?

"She who avoids will soon be seeking;
Who gives back gifts will be giving hers;

Who does not love will soon be in love,
    If unwillingly."

Come once more! This hard-to-be-dealt-with
Anxiety loosen, and what my
Spirit would have let it have, yourself
    My fellow–soldier.

[LP, Fr. 31]

He is, I should say, on a level
With deity, the man who sits over
Against you, and attends to the nearby
Sweetness of your voice

And charm of your laughter. I tell you
It frightens the quick heart in my breast.
For, soon as I look at you, there is
No voice left to me,

My tongue has been fractured, a thin fire
Instantly runs underneath my skin.
My eyes cannot see anything, and
My ears re-echo.

I am in a cold sweat, a trembling
Seizes me all over, and, pallid
As range grass, I think I am almost
On the point of death.

[LP, Fr. 130]

Love strikes me again, that makes the legs give way,
That sweet-bitter, not-to-be-fought-with shape.

[LP, Fr. 147]

Someone I tell you will remember us.

Deduke men a selanna

(formerly attributed to Sappho)

The moon has set now, and
The Pleiades. It is
Midnight, the hours go by,
And I lie here alone.

DECIMUS LABERIUS

An Old Actor Addresses Julius Caesar

Necessity, the impact of whose sidelong course
Many attempt to escape and only few succeed,
Whither have you thrust down, almost to his wits' ends,
Him whom flattery, whom never bribery
Could in his youth avail to shake him from his stand?
But see how easily an old man slips, and shows,
Moved by the complacency of this most excellent man,
Calm and complaisant, a submissive, fawning speech!
Yet naught to a conqueror could the gods themselves deny,
And who then would permit one man to say him nay?
I who existed sixty long years without stain,
A Roman Knight who went from his paternal gods,
Now return home a mime. And certainly today
I've lived out one more day than I should have lived.
Fortune, unrestrained in prosperity and ill,
Were it your pleasure with the lure and praise of letters
To shatter the very summit of my good name,
Why when I prospered, when my limbs were green with youth,
When I could satisfy an audience and such a man,
Did you not bend my suppleness and spit on me?
Now you cast me? Whither? What brought I to the stage?
The ornament of beauty, dignity of flesh,
Fire of the spirit, the music of a pleasing voice?
As twining ivy kills the stout heart of the tree,
So has senility in time's embrace destroyed me,
And like a sepulchre I keep only a name.

CATULLUS 85

I hate and love her. If you ask me why
I don't know. But I feel it and am torn.

HORACE

Odes 1.9

See how resplendent in deep snow
Soracte stands, how straining trees
    Scarce can sustain their burden
        Now that the rivers congeal and freeze.

Thaw out the chill, still heaping more
Wood on the hearth; ungrudgingly
    Pour forth from Sabine flagons,
        O Thaliarchus, the ripened wine.

Leave all else to the gods. They soon
Will level on the yeasty deep
    Th' embattled tempests, stirring
        Cypress no more, nor agèd ash.

Tomorrow may no man divine.
This day that Fortune gives set down
    As profit, nor while young still
        Scorn the rewards of sweet dancing love,

So long as from your flowering days
Crabbed age delays. Now through the parks

Soft whisperings toward nightfall
    Visit again at the trysting hour;

Now from her bower comes the charmed laugh,
Betrayer of the hiding girl;
    Now from her arm the forfeit
        Plundered, her fingers resisting not.

MARTIAL

1.32

Sabinus, I don't like you. You know why?
Sabinus, I don't like you. That is why.

1.33

In private she mourns not the late-lamented;
If someone's by, her tears leap forth on call.
Sorrow, my dear, is not so easily rented.
They are true tears that without witness fall.

2.4

Bert is beguiling with his mother,
She is beguiling with her Bert.
They call each other *Sister, Brother,*
And others call them something other.
Is it no fun to be yourselves?
Or is this fun? I'd say it's not.

A mother who would be a sister
Would be no mother and no sister.

2.5

Believe me, sir, I'd like to spend whole days,
Yes, and whole evenings in your company,
But the two miles between your house and mine
Are four miles when I go there to come back.
You're seldom home, and when you are deny it,
Engrossed with business or with yourself.
Now, I don't mind the two-mile trip to see you;
What I do mind is going four to not to.

2.55

You would be courted, dear, and I would love you.
But be it as you will, and I will court you.
But if I court you, dear, I will not love you.

2.68

That I now call you by your name
Who used to call you sir and master,
You needn't think it impudence.
I bought myself with all I had.
He ought to sir a sir and master
Who's not himself, and wants to have
Whatever sirs and masters want.
Who can get by without a slave
Can get by, too, without a master.

4.33

You write, you tell me, for posterity.
May you be read, my friend, immediately.

4.69

You serve the best wines always, my dear sir,
And yet they say your wines are not so good.
They say you are four times a widower.
They say . . . A drink? I don't believe I would.

6.65

"An epic epigram," I heard you say.
Others have written them, and so I may.
"But this one is too long." Others are too.
You want them short? I'll write two lines for you:
  As for long epigrams let us agree
  They may be skipped by you, written by me.

STATIUS

Siluae 5.4: On Sleep

What was my crime, youthful most gentle god,
What folly was it that I alone should lack,
Sweet Sleep, thy gifts? All herds, birds, beasts are still,
The curved mountains seem wearily asleep,
Streams rage with muted noise, the sea-wave falls,
And the still-nodding deep rests on the shore.
Seven times now returning Phoebe sees
My sick eyes stare, and so the morning star
And evening, so Tithonia glides by
My tears, sprinkling sad dew from her cool whip.
How, then, may I endure? Not though were mine
The thousand eyes wherewith good Argus kept
But shifting watch, nor all his flesh awake.
But now, alas! If this long night some lover
In his girl's arms should willingly repel thee,
Thence come sweet Sleep! Nor with all thy power
Pour through my eyes—so may they ask, the many,
More happy—; touch me with thy wand's last tip,
Enough, or lightly pass with hovering step.

HADRIAN

My little soul, my vagrant charmer,
The friend and house-guest of this matter,
Where will you now be visitor
In naked pallor, little soul,
And not so witty as you were?

SAINT AMBROSE

Aeterne Rerum Conditor

Builder eternally of things,
Thou rulest over night and day,
Disposing time in separate times
That Thou mayst lessen weariness;

Now crows the herald of the day,
Watchful throughout the wasting dark,
To walkers in the night a clock
Marking the hours of dark and dawn.

The morning star arises now
To free the obscure firmament;
Now every gang and prowling doom
Forsakes the dark highways of harm.

The sailor now regathers strength,
The channels of the sea grow calm;
And now Peter, the living rock,
Washes his guilt in the last crow.

Then quickly let us rise and go;
The cock stirs up the sleepy-head,
And chides again the lie-a-bed;
The cock convicts them who deny.

And to cock-crow our hopes reply;
Thy grace refills our ailing hearts;
The sword of brigandage is hid;
And faith returns where faith had fled.

Jesu, look back on us who fall,
Straighten the conduct of our life;
If Thou lookst back, denials fail,
And guilt is melted in a tear.

Thou Light, illumine with Thy light
Our sleeping lethargy of soul;
Thy name the first our lips shall choose,
Discharging thus our vows to Thee.

THE ARCHPOET

The Confession of Bishop Golias

Inwardly fired with vehement wrath,
In bitterness I will speak my mind;
Made of material light as lath,
I am like a leaf tossed by the wind.

Though it were just for the wise and brave
To place their seat on the rock of will,
Fool, I am like the flowing wave
That under one sky is ever unstill.

I am borne on as a pilotless ship,
As a vagrant bird through the cloudy haze;
Ungoverned by reins, ungoverned by whip,
I gad with my kind, I follow their ways.

I walk the broad path in the fashion of youth,
Forgetful of virtue, entangled with sin;

Avid of pleasure more than of truth
I die in soul but take care of my skin.

Most worthy prelate, I pray your pardon,
I die a good death, swing on a sweet rope,
At sight of the ladies I still get a hard on,
Whom I cannot by touch, I sin with in hope.

Who placed on a pyre will not burn in the fire?
Or dallying at Pavia can keep himself chaste?
Where Venus goes hunting young men for hire,
Drooping her eyelids and fixing her face.

Hippolytus placed in Pavia today
Would not be Hippolytus "when the dawn came";
To the bedroom of Venus still runs the broad way,
Nor in all those towers is the tower of shame.

Again, I'm charged with playing strip poker:
When play casts me out in my naked skin,
Shivering, I sweat while my mind plays stoker,
And I write better verse than I did within.

The tavern, thirdly, I note in this summing
Up of the life I will ever have led
Till I hear the holy angels coming,
Singing rest eternal unto the dead;

For I propose in the tavern to die
That wine may be near when the throat grows hard,
And the chorus of angels may joyfully cry,
"O Lord, be kindly to this drunkard."

The lamp of the soul is lighted by wine,
Sotted with nectar it flies to the sky;

Wine of the tavern is far more divine
Than watery wine that the priest raises high.

They say a poet should flee public places
And choose his seat in a quiet retreat:
He sweats, presses on, stays awake, and erases,
Yet comes back with scarcely one clear conceit.

The chorus of poets should fast and abstain,
Avoid public quarrels and brawls with their neighbors:
That they may compose what will ever remain,
They die in a cell, overcome by their labours.

Nature to such gives a suitable crown:
I never could write on an empty purse;
Myself when fasting a boy could knock down;
Thirsting and hunger I hate like a hearse.

Never's the spirit of poetry given
Except when the belly is fat and sleek;
While Bacchus is lord of my cerebral heaven,
Apollo moves through me and marvels I speak.

Behold, of my vice I was that informer
By whom your henchmen indicted me;
No one of them is his own accuser,
Though he hopes to sport through eternity.

So I stand before the blessed prelate
Urging that precept of our Lord wherein
He casts the first stone, nor spares the poet,
Whose heart is wholly devoid of sin.

I've charged myself with whatever I knew
And vomited up my long cherished dole;

The old life passes, gives way to the new;
Man notes appearance, Jove sees the soul.

Primate of Cologne, grant me your blessing,
Absolve the sinner who begs your grace;
Impose due penance on him confessing;
Whatever you bid I'll gladly embrace.

PIETRO BEMBO

On Raphael

This is that Raphael the Great Source of All
Feared as Its master, with his fall to fall.

JANUS VITALIS PANORMITANUS

Rome

You that a stranger in mid-Rome seek Rome
And can find nothing in mid-Rome of Rome,
Behold this mass of walls, these abrupt rocks,
Where the vast theatre lies overwhelmed.
Here, here is Rome! Look how the very corpse
Of greatness still imperiously breathes threats!
The world she conquered, strove herself to conquer,
Conquered that nothing be unconquered by her.
Now conqueror Rome's interred in conquered Rome,
And the same Rome conquered and conqueror.

Still Tiber stays, witness of Roman fame,
Still Tiber flows on swift waves to the sea.
Learn hence what Fortune can: the unmoved falls
And the ever-moving will remain forever.

THOMAS MORE

The Astrologer

What is it, fool, in the tall stars you'd find
About the earthy morals of your spouse?
Why search so far? Your fears are close at hand.
For while you polled the poles for what she'd do
She did it willingly and on the ground.

GEORGE BUCHANAN

1.

The Pope from penance purgatorial
Freed some, but Martin Luther freed them all.

2.

Neaera when I'm there is adamant,
And when I'm not there is annoyed,
And not from tenderness and sentiment
But that my pain is unenjoyed.

3.

Rome conquered earth with arms, the sea with ships,
Till the world's limits were the city limits.
Only the otherworlds remained. The faith
Of the first Pontiffs shattered old Olympus,
And their posterity, adventurous
As they, hasten to Hell in hotfoot haste.

Abbreviations

TH	Cunningham, *The Helmsman*, 1942
JF	Cunningham, *The Judge Is Fury*, 1947
DD	Cunningham, *Doctor Drink*, 1950
TVE	Cunningham, *Trivial, Vulgar, and Exalted*, 1957
TPS	Cunningham, *Tradition and Poetic Structure: Essays in Literary History and Criticism*, 1960
ER	Cunningham, *The Exclusions of a Rhyme*, 1960
TWSWW	Cunningham, *To What Strangers, What Welcome*, 1964
LL	Cunningham, *Latin Lines*, 1965
SS	Cunningham, *Some Salt*, 1967
CPE	*The Collected Poems and Epigrams of J. V. Cunningham*, 1971
CE	*The Collected Essays of J. V. Cunningham*, 1976
LTWBF	Cunningham, *Let Thy Words Be Few*, 1988
Gullans	Charles Gullans, *A Bibliography of the Published Works of J. V. Cunningham 1931-1988*, revised and enlarged (Florence, Kentucky: Robert L. Barth, 1988)
OED	*The Oxford English Dictionary*, with supplement and bibliography, 1971
YSW	*Yearbook of Stanford Writing*, 1932–1937

Selected Bibliography

Barth, R. L. "The Vacancies of Need: Particularity in J.V. Cunningham's *To What Strangers, What Welcome.*" *The Southern Review* 18 (Spring 1982), 286–98.

Baxter, John. "The Province of the Plain Style." *The Compass* 3 (Spring 1978), 15–37.

Chicago Review 35 (Autumn 1985). This contains memorial essays on Cunningham by W. S. DiPiero, Kenneth Fields, Robert Pinsky, and Alan Shapiro and memorial poems by Thom Gunn and Raymond Oliver. Pinsky's essay is a reprinting of the item listed below under his name. Shapiro's essay is reprinted in his *In Praise of the Impure,* also listed below. It is the second of the items mentioned there.

Dickey, James. "J.V. Cunningham," in Dickey's *Babel to Byzantium* (New York: Farrar Straus, 1968), 193–94.

Donoghue, Denis. "Edwin Arlington Robinson, J. V. Cunningham, Robert Lowell," in Donoghue's *Connoisseurs of Chaos* (New York: MacMillan, 1965), 129–59.

Fields, Kenneth. "J.V. Cunningham and Others." *The Southern Review* 5 (Spring 1969), 563–81.

Fraser, John. "Heroic Order in the Poetry of J.V. Cunningham." *The Southern Review* 23 (Winter 1987), 68–83.

Helmling, Steven. "J.V. Cunningham," *Dictionary of Literary Biography,* vol. 5, part 1 (Detroit: Gale, 1980), 159–65.

Hill, Jack. "J.V. Cunningham's Roman Voices," in R. W. Butterfield, ed. *Modern American Poetry* (Totowa, New Jersey: Barnes and Noble, 1984), 173–86.

Hooley, Daniel M. "Some Notes on Translation: Martial and J.V. Cunningham." *Classical and Modern Literature* 3 (Summer 1983), 181–91.

Kaye, Frances W. "The West as Desolation: J.V. Cunningham's *To What Strangers, What Welcome.*" *The Southern Review* 11 (Autumn 1975), 820–24.

Oliver, Raymond. "'The Scholar is a Mere Conservative': The Criticism of J.V. Cunningham." *The Southern Review* 15 (Summer 1979), 545–59.

Pinsky, Robert. "The Poetry of J.V. Cunningham." *The New Republic* 178 (January 28, 1978), 25–26, 28–29.

Sequoia 29 (Spring 1985). This contains memorial essays about Cunningham by John Baxter, Edgar Bowers, Kenneth Fields, and Timothy Steele, as well as an excerpt, discussing Cunningham, from Irving Howe's *A Margin of Hope: An Intellectual Autobiography* (New York: Harcourt Brace, 1982).

Shankman, Steven. "J. V. Cunningham's 'Montana Pastoral' and the Pastoral Tradition," in Shankman's *In Search of the Classic* (University Park, Penn.: Pennsylvania State University Press, 1995), 205–13.

Shapiro, Alan. "'Far Lamps at Night': The Poetry of J. V. Cunningham" and "The Early Seventies and J. V. Cunningham" in Shapiro's *In Praise of the Impure* (Evanston: TriQuarterly Books, 1993), pp. 93–113, 182–85.

Stall, Lindon. "The Trivial, Vulgar, and Exalted: The Poems of J. V. Cunningham." *The Southern Review* 9 (Autumn 1973), 1044–48.

Steele, Timothy. "An Interview with J. V. Cunningham." *The Iowa Review* 15 (Fall 1985), pp. 1–24.

Taylor, Henry. "J. V. Cunningham: The Last Variation is Regularity," in Taylor's *Compulsory Figures* (Baton Rouge: Louisiana State University Press, 1992), 1–17.

Winters, Yvor. *The Poetry of J. V. Cunningham* (Denver: Swallow, 1961). The material in this essay-pamphlet appears, revised and abridged, in Winters's *Forms of Discovery* (Denver: Swallow, 1967), 299–311.

Commentary

Much of the following commentary consists of Cunningham's own remarks about his poetry. These appear mainly in three essays: "The Quest of the Opal," "The Journal of John Cardan," and "Several Kinds of Short Poem." Anyone interested in the poet will find these essays fascinating, and it might seem logical to reprint them in their entirety as an appendix to this book. This material, however, runs to thirty-five closely printed pages in Cunningham's *Collected Essays,* and Cunningham speaks not only of his poems, but also of other concerns. Further, even when in "The Quest of the Opal" he speaks more or less exclusively of his work, he skips around among poems: he does not follow any sequence related to the order in which they appear in his collections. One must do a good deal of rummaging to correlate poems with the essay passages that discuss them. And though Cunningham comments on most of the more difficult early poems, he does not speak of them all. With only the essays at hand, one may wind up searching for explications of works about which Cunningham says nothing.

Hence in my notes I have extracted passages from Cunningham's essays and keyed these excerpts to the poems they address. This will enable readers readily to find Cunningham's comments, when such exist, on this or that poem. Also, readers will be able to see, alongside Cunningham's discussion, whatever editorial annotations may be applicable to the poem. Thus all the supporting information for any given title will be in one place. (Readers are reminded that Cunningham, in his autocritical writings, generally refers to himself in the third person. And unless it is otherwise indicated, I am responsible for the translations in the notes.)

I should explain the place-and-date-of-composition data that appear in this commentary. The data derive chiefly from two sources. The first is a copy of *The Collected Poems and Epigrams* which Cunningham owned and in which he entered, in blue ink below the poems, where and when they were written. In a few cases, Cunningham's memory failed him, and a question mark appears under a poem. The second source is Charles Gullans's *Bibliography* of Cunningham's work. In an appendix to this bibliography, Gullans places and dates the composition not only of most of the poems, but also of some of the translations.

(Cunningham does not in his copy of *CPE* give such data for his translations.) Gullans lists as well the places and dates of composition for poems that appeared in Cunningham's earlier books but that were dropped from *CPE*. Generally, the information supplied by Cunningham harmonizes with that given by Gullans, but occasional inconsistencies crop up. Where these occur, my notes register and, when possible, resolve them.

Some might reasonably ask why, apart from citing Gullans's data about the translations and the poems dropped from *CPE*, I have attended to his information about the rest of the poetry when Cunningham himself speaks so directly on the subject. The answer is that *The Collected Poems and Epigrams* is a late volume: it was published in 1971, and Cunningham's notes in his copy of it (he dates the book May 18, 1971) are likewise late. It is conceivable that when he made these late notes he was drawing on earlier ones, but so far as I have been able to determine, there is no evidence that this was the case. In contrast, for his *Bibliography*, Gullans consulted presentation copies of earlier collections—including *The Helmsman* and *The Exclusions of a Rhyme*—in which Cunningham had recorded for their owners where and when the poems were written. According to comments that Gullans wrote on the endpaper of his own working copy of *The Exclusions of a Rhyme*, the notes in the copy of *TH* date from circa 1943, and the notes in the copy of *ER* date from 1964. Moreover, Cunningham checked the place-and-date-of-composition data in Gullans's *Bibliography* when it appeared in 1973 and subsequently made corrections (Gullans, v) which were incorporated in the revised edition of the bibliography. So Gullans's work reflects both pre- and post-1971 testimony from the poet. On this ground alone, it merits serious consideration.

In reference to the place-and date-of-composition data, I should add that the amount of information varies from title to title. In some cases, Cunningham specified the place and the day that he wrote a poem. In other cases, he specified a month, season, or year, but could not or at least did not pinpoint where or when during that period he wrote it. In yet other cases, he could assign no more than a very approximate date (e.g., "1933 or 1934") to something he had written.

Sometimes Cunningham lists, in connection with a poem's composition, two dates. For instance, for "The Symposium," he notes "Dec. '33, Winter '36." In such cases, I have construed the first date as when the poem was begun and the second as when it was completed. I do not mean to suggest, however, that a continuous, slowly incremental process was necessarily involved. On a number of occasions, Cunningham wrote a poem and published it in a magazine, only to re-work it extensively later. He once said: "When I began writing, I did a good deal not merely of rewriting, but of smashing an original version to pieces and doing it completely over, maybe several times" (Steele, "An Interview with J. V. Cunningham," 23). And with certain double datings (see for example, the note below for "The Predestined Space"), the earlier date evidently marks a time when Cunningham wrote something that seemed finished and the later date a time when he decided to re-cast the poem.

To the dates of ten poems, Cunningham appended one or two plus signs. For example, for "In Innocence" he wrote "Aug. '31++" and for "The Chase" he noted "Spring '34+." These plus signs are a mystery. I suspect that Cunningham intended them to signify subsequent revision, but did not employ them in a consistent manner. Of the ten poems in question, eight received fairly thorough revision after they first appeared in magazines; and several had their titles changed. But Cunningham did not attach plus signs to the dates of other poems that he had similarly revised. Whatever the meaning of the plus signs, my notes indicate where they occur; a reader cleverer than I may discern a pattern I have missed.

On a more general point, I should say that most of Cunningham's best poems are clear without commentary. The amount of annotation that a poem receives does not indicate a recommendation of it at the expense of a little-glossed or unglossed title. As was observed in the introduction, Cunningham undertook a commentary on his early poems precisely because he recognized that they were not always successful on their own terms.

Nor, for that matter, need readers pay attention to this commentary unless they so wish. Here, as in all such cases, Samuel Johnson's remarks on commentary are apposite:

> Notes are often necessary, but they are necessary evils. . . . Particular passages are cleared by notes, but the general effect of the work is weakened. The mind is re-frigerated by interruption; the thoughts are diverted from the principal subject; the reader is weary, he suspects not why; and at last throws away the book which he has too diligently studied. ("Preface to the Edition of Shakespeare's Plays," in *Samuel Johnson on Shakespeare,* edited with an introduction and notes by H. R. Woudhuysen [London: Penguin, 1989], 163–64)

The Helmsman (1942)

Epigraph to The Helmsman *("Of Thirty Years . . .")*

Written in Los Altos, California, in 1941, to preface *The Helmsman,* which appeared from the Colt Press in January 1942.

Lector Aere Perennior

Written in Stanford, California, in December 1933. (To prevent confusion about the location, one should note that Stanford surrounds and incorporates the university of the same name; it is, in other words, an actual community, though it is often mistakenly reported that the school is in Palo Alto and though it is commonly assumed that any reference to Stanford must be to the campus proper.) The poem's title translates as "The Reader More Enduring Than Bronze" and alludes to Horace's statement (*Odes,* 3.30.1) about his poems: *Exegi monumentum aere perennius* ("I have completed a monument more enduring than bronze"). In contrast to Horace's confidence, Cunningham suggests that poets survive only by means of sympathetic readers, who read poetry in the spirit of the person who wrote it. As Cunningham says:

> We are told that the immortality of a writer consists in the fact that his name lives. Yet . . . [i]nsofar as he continues in a recurrent existence he lives as the text of his writings. This is the inert clay which a sympathetic reader can inform with the breath of existence if he has the irrational trick of assuming the spirit of the author, of inviting a kind of transmigration of soul. The text only is constant, but in this reader or that it may come to life again with the soul of its original meaning. . . . The author dies; his text is inert; the reader is his life. (*CE,* 409)

8 Pythagoras: A Greek philosopher (c. 582–c. 500 B.C.) who believed in metempsychosis, the transmigration and reincarnation of souls after death. On Pythagoras, see also the note to "The Man of Feeling."

The Wandering Scholar's Prayer to Saint Catherine of Egypt

Written in Palo Alto, California, in winter 1932. According to legend, Saint Catherine of Alexandria was a Christian martyr of the early fourth century. During persecutions conducted by the emperor Maxentius, she was condemned to be racked on a wheel, which, however, miraculously broke after she was set on it. When the emperor then had her decapitated, milk rather than blood is reported to have flowed from her body. Because of her learning and of her refutation and conversion of the fifty pagan philosophers with whom Maxentius confronted her in public debate, Catherine became the patron saint of scholars. The phrase "Wandering Scholar" alludes to the *vagantes,* the itinerant goliardic scholar-poets of the late medieval period. Kenneth Fields once suggested in conversation that Cunningham's poem may have been influenced by *The Wandering Scholars* by Helen Waddell, which was first published in 1927 and was long a popular book on the subject. Fields's suggestion is supported by the fact that at the time Cunningham wrote "The Wandering Scholar's Prayer," he was interested in medieval Latin verse and translated the "Confession" of the Archpoet, a figure to whom Waddell devotes a chapter of her book. Of "The Wandering Scholar's Prayer," Cunningham writes: "The structure of the poem was in part a device for alluding to jagged bits of experience. . . . [T]he subject of the poem is the loss or betrayal of all one's early loyalties" (*CE,* 418).

12 Dying with Swift in idiot froth: For much of his life, Jonathan Swift (1667–1745) suffered periodically from vertigo. Modern scholarship suspects that the cause was Ménière's syndrome. The effects of the malady intensified as Swift aged. Many considered him insane, and in 1742 the courts judged him mentally incompetent and appointed guardians for him. Cunningham's line echoes Samuel Johnson's comment ("Vanity of Human Wishes," 318), "And Swift expires a driv'ler and a show." Additional comment on Swift appears below in the note to "With a Copy of Swift's Works." **14 ravelled:** Cunningham comments on this "Hart Crane-ish violence of epithet ('the ravelled faces of the park' are unshaven)" (*CE,* 418).

The Dogdays

Written in Palo Alto in summer 1932. Of "Dog-days," the *OED* says: "The days about the time of the heliacal rising of the Dog-star [Sirius or Canicula]; noted from ancient times as the hottest and most unwholesome period of the year. . . . *fig.* An evil time; a period in which malignant influences prevail." Partly owing to the precession of the equinoxes, the dogdays now occur a little later in the year than they did in antiquity. According to current almanacs, they run from July 3 to August 11. The poem's epigraph comes from Horace (*Odes,* 1.17.17-18): "Here in this retired valley, you'll shelter from Canicula's heat." A discussion of the poem may be found in the introduction to this book.

Elegy for a Cricket

Written in Palo Alto in spring 1933. The epigraph comes from Catullus (3.13-14): "But a curse on you, evil shadows / Of Orcus, which devour all that is beautiful." Cunningham's poem resembles Catullus's, in that both are elegies for small creatures. (Catullus's concerns his lover's sparrow.) Cunningham also adopts the metrical form, Phalaecean hendecasyllabics, that Catullus uses. The meter in Catullus consists of the sequence, trochee-dactyl-trochee-trochee-trochee, with these possible variations: in the first foot, either syllable may be long or short, and in the final trochee, the second syllable may be long or short. Ancient prosody measures syllabic length, whereas modern English prosody is based on syllabic stress; and rather than trying to measure the lengths of his syllables, Cunningham simply places beats where Catullus has long syllables and off-beats where Catullus has short.

5 Dis: Another name for "Pluto," Roman god of the Underworld. **6 whirling throng of lovers:** An allusion to Dante's *Inferno,* 5.31-33, which depicts the souls of the lustful being blown about the Second Circle of Hell by a "terrible gale . . . spinning and striking" (*bufera infernal . . . voltando e percotendo*).

All Choice Is Error

Written in Palo Alto in winter 1933. When Cunningham initially published this poem (*YSW* 4 [June 1933] and *Hound and Horn* 9 [October–December 1933]), he entitled it "Our Lady of the Night." He changed the title to "Dream Vision" for *TH* and *ER.* The poem first appeared under its current title in *CPE.* The poem concerns, in Cunningham's words,

> the notion of particularity and of choice, and especially the formula which has shocked everyone that ever stopped to look at it, as it shocked him: "All choice is error." For choice implies exclusion, rejection, restriction, limitation. To choose *this* is not only to prefer one thing to something else, but rather to prefer it to everything else. (*CE,* 412)

For discussion of this theme in Cunningham's work in general, see Introduction.

9-10 Europa, Iö, Danaë: Mythical mortal women with whom Zeus had affairs. In the form of a bull, he abducted Europa, carrying her across the sea to Crete from her home in the Asia Minor city of Tyre. Iö was the daughter of the river-god Inachus. Attempting to hide from Hera his affair with Iö, Zeus turned her into a heifer, but Hera saw through the disguise and plagued Iö with the gadfly. Eventually, after she had wandered to Egypt, Zeus restored her humanity. Danaë's father, Acrisius, sequestered her in a tower to keep her away from men because it had been prophesied that he would be killed by a son of hers. Zeus visited the imprisoned maiden in a shower of gold. As a result of this encounter, Danaë gave birth to Perseus, who did kill Acrisius, accidentally braining him with a discus during an athletic festival in Thessaly. **21–23 Kiss, then, . . . A leaf's weight up and down:** In his working copy of *ER,* Gullans has tipped in, at the page with "Dream Vision" (one of the earlier titles of "All Choice Is Error"), a slip of 4" x 5 1/2" yellow paper with this note: "All choice is error. Metaphysical assertion but we choose whom we love in the face of that knowledge & tho it affects eternity minutely—a leaf's weight up or down—it still affects it."

Obsequies for a Poetess

Written in Palo Alto in summer 1933. When this poem first appeared in *Hound and Horn* 7 (October–December 1933), it was subtitled "Kathleen Tankersley Young, obit 1933." Young published verse in *Hound and Horn, Blues, Poetry,* and other journals. In 1932, Angel Flores's Dragon Press issued a collection of her work, *The Dark Land.* She and Cunningham apparently did not know each other personally. He briefly spoke of her in a round-up review of ten poets (*Commonweal* 16 [October 5, 1932], 541), characterizing her work as "sensitive minor poetry, completely subjective but without self-pity." He may have dropped the subtitle with her name because her style, which is influenced principally by Eliot and Joyce, is not consonant with the poem's allusions to Beardsley and Dowson and to the mannerisms of fin-de-siècle art.

   9–10 Aubrey . . . Dowson: The artist Aubrey Vincent Beardsley (1872-1898) and the poet Ernest Christopher Dowson (1867-1900) were, along with Oscar Wilde, among the leading figures in the art-for-art's-sake movement in England in the 1890s.

The Symposium

Begun in Stanford in December 1933 and finished in Palo Alto in winter 1936.

   9–11 the new . . . social view: A reference to the movement in literary criticism in the 1930s that demanded that poetry be socially relevant. It is interesting that the year that Cunningham completed this poem saw the publication of Stevens's *Ideas of Order* and Frost's *A Further Range,* both of which were severely attacked for not addressing social and political issues. **14–16 clarity . . . propriety:** Evidently an allusion to Aristotle's comment (*Rhetoric*, 3.2.1–2) that virtue or excellence in speech *(lexeōs aretē)* consists of clarity *(saphē),* informed by a sense of propriety *(to prepon,* i.e., a tactful suiting of style to subject).

The Beacon

Written in Denver in spring 1934. For discussion of this poem, see Introduction. Also, a fine analysis of the poem appears in Shapiro, *In Praise of the Impure,* 105–6.

Fancy

Written in Denver in June 1934. The title of the poem refers simply to the creative faculty. Cunningham is not drawing a Coleridgean distinction between Fancy and Imagination. This is one of several of Cunningham's poems that advocate a middle way between extremes. If the creative faculty is totally unchecked ("free-reined"), it will run amok. But if it is overly restrained ("untimely stayed") by pure intellect ("passionless mind"), it will be sterile. The meter of the poem is, as Cunningham states in "The Quest of the Opal," purely accentual: "each line should have four accents and . . . there should be no regular pattern of feet" (*CE,* 419).

  6; 10 still: The word is used in the old sense of "always, ever."

The Helmsman: An Ode

Written in Denver in May or June 1934. (Cunningham gives the former month, Gullans the latter, as the time of composition.) Cunningham's extensive comments on the poem connect it with his own experience during the Depression:

> The normal course of a man's life, we are told, is through experience to maturity—to poise, assurance, mastery. The traditional term is wisdom. But such mastery, if in fact it visit us, is only accidental to the process of living, and is at the best casual, fitful, and dependent upon some source of illumination external to the inner personality. Furthermore, it presupposes normal, comfortable, easy circumstances; it is a consequence of good weather. But time may fail us, the loves that render such accomplishment possible may die or disappoint us, so that the very idea of fulfillment is only a childhood memory. There is a certain degree of want and loss, varying with circumstance, that destroys a man's self-respect. So he

goes his own way, though the vision of what might have been intrudes from time to time like an importunate panhandler. He cuts free of the past—Ajax and the Grecian isles—putting out his last reserves for a special dinner and a pint of bootleg, and sets forth on his travels. If ever he should feel secure, he will drowse and fall from the wheel like Aeneas' helmsman, Palinurus, whose unburied bones will finally wash up on some unknown shore. (*CE,* 420–21)

Of the poem's form, Cunningham says that it is

an attempt to imitate the Horatian ode. . . . The meter of the poem was intended to achieve in English the effect of the Alcaic strophe. It consisted of four lines, each of a different metrical pattern, so that the strophe stood out as a unit without the use of rhyme, though rhyme was admitted here and there as a figure of diction. (*CE,* 418–19)

18–20 Ajax . . . Teucer: Teucer is the master-archer and half-brother of the greater Ajax, alongside whom he fights (e.g., *Iliad,* 8.266 ff.; 12.370 ff.) in the Trojan War. In Sophocles' *Ajax,* Teucer leads the struggle to secure the body of Ajax an honorable burial after the latter has gone mad and committed suicide on account of the Greeks' having awarded not him but Odysseus the fallen Achilles' armor. According to legend, when Teucer returned home to Salamis, he was banished by his father Telemon for not having brought Ajax back with him. Hence, Teucer's having to leave, in Cunningham's poem, "his friends and kin." **20–28:** As Cunningham notes (*CE,* 421), these lines draw on Horace's Ode 1.7.21–32, which tells of Teucer's banishment, and on Virgil's account of Palinurus, who falls asleep one night while steering his ship and tumbles overboard; Cunningham's last three lines adapt Aeneas's lament for Palinurus (*Aeneid,* 5.870–71):

> o nimium caelo et pelago confise sereno,
> nudus in ignota, Palinure, iacebis harena.

O excessively confident of the calm sky and sea, naked on an unknown shore, Palinurus, you lie.

Hymn in Adversity

Written in Denver in spring 1934. (In Gullans, this title is mistakenly double-listed, with first Stanford and then Denver given for the place of composition; in Gullans's working copy of *CPE,* as in Cunningham's copy of *CPE,* Denver is recorded as where the poem was written.) In March of 1934, Cunningham graduated with his A.B. from Stanford and returned to Denver, where his mother was dying of cancer. This circumstance may explain the bleak tone of this poem, of the preceding poem, and of the following poem—and the concern in all of these poems with family tradition.

A Moral Poem

Written in Denver in spring 1934. About the poem, Cunningham comments:

> The tradition that surrounded him and formed much of the texture of his early years was the tradition of Irish Catholics along the railroads of the West. To this he finally bade such farewell as one can to his past in *A Moral Poem*. So far as a man's traditions are himself they cannot be altered but they need not be exploited. He who is inured to the past is at liberty to be what he becomes. (*CE*, 421)

Cunningham also notes that the poem was written in "syllabic meter . . . in which the principle was that each line should consist of five syllables and that there should be no regular pattern of feet" (*CE*, 419).

15 Nor live curiously: The adverb is used in the sense of the Latin *curiose,* "carefully, taking pains and precautions (even to a fault)." One should, Cunningham is saying here and in the next line, leave something to chance, to providence.

Timor Dei

According to Gullans, written in Los Altos, California, in spring 1938. (Cunningham notes in his copy of *CPE* simply "'38? | Los Altos.") The title is Latin for "Fear of God." The poem's first six lines are a variation on the opening of Charles Baudelaire's "Hymne." (Cunningham himself pointed out this source, as well the sources for several other poems—see Gullans, v–vi.) Though Baudelaire's is a love poem, it is addressed to Apollonnie Sabatier, whom he associated with spiritual as opposed to physical love. Hence the feeling in Baudelaire's poem is, as its title suggests, devotional. While Cunningham draws on Baudelaire, the skeptical tone of "Timor Dei" contrasts with the worshipful tone of "Hymne":

> À la très-chère, à la très-belle
> Qui remplit mon coeur de clarté,
> À l'ange, à l'idole immortelle
> Salut en l'immortalité!

Elle se répand dans ma vie
Comme un air imprégné de sel . . .

To the most dear, to the most beautiful, who fills my soul with clarity, to the angel, to the immortal idol, hail in immortality! She spreads herself through my life like air permeated with salt . . .

After following Baudelaire's "Hymne" for six lines, "Timor Dei" then goes its own way. Cunningham writes of the poem:

> He dealt with the specific problem of his religious inheritance in *Timor Dei*. He was a Catholic by tradition, training, and deep feeling, but the Absolute is greedy, as pervasive and as destructively absorbent as sensation or passion or sympathy. Hence his own identity he fenced off, and though it formed part of the terrain it had its property lines. Yet he could look back to the smoke of burning leaves and grass, of the swinging censers, and of breath in the chill northern air of his boyhood and almost acquiesce: for though he would not regret the loss of what he would not have, the traditional patterns of feeling still had power to dominate him. (*CE,* 421)

Choice

Begun in Los Altos in 1937 (?)—the question mark is Cunningham's—and completed in Los Altos in 1939. In "The Journal of John Cardan," Cunningham paraphrases the poem:

> Where the issue of our commitments denies even a reasonable fulfillment to our desires we must act in accordance with the commitment, even to the extent of effectively pretending that we enjoy what cannot be altered. We can do this without in the least denying the existence, or the validity, or even the power of desire. So we save ourselves from the sentimental death of the heart, and at the same time protect ourselves from engrossment in our wayward wishes. For a man must live divided against himself: only the selfishly insane can integrate experience to the heart's desire, and only the emotionally sterile would not wish to. (*CE,* 426)

Summer Idyll

Written in Los Altos in summer 1939. Cunningham describes this poem as an attempt to convey "the lethargic resignation . . . the rather terrible inertia of a late June afternoon when the ripe apricots fall in the sullen orchard with a foreboding sound" (*CE,* 414). Cunningham adds that the poem indicates that the program of emotional adjustment that "Choice" recommended "did not in this instance work out too well" (*CE,* 414). *CPE* places "Summer Idyll" after "Choice" (in *TH* and *ER* the order was reversed). In this one case I have followed the *CPE* sequence on the grounds that it is more illuminating than the earlier arrangement.

For My Contemporaries

Written in Los Altos in May 1939. This poem addresses the distinction between poetry and verse. (This distinction has a long history and is discussed in the third chapter of my *Missing Measures: Modern Poetry and the Revolt against Meter* [Fayetteville, Ark.: University of Arkansas Press, 1990]). Ever since the ancient Greeks, writers and readers have debated whether poetic art owes its distinctive character to its metrical element or to some more general quality, such as fiction or sublimity or vivid emotion. In the last two hundred years or so, the latter position has been almost universally adopted. And twentieth-century critics (e.g., T. S. Eliot) often depreciate technically competent verse in favor of a poetry that is less formally defined but is felt to be more essentially vital. Of this poem and of the personal orientation it expresses, Cunningham says:

> [H]e viewed himself rather as a professional writer, however laconic, one to whom poetry was verse.
>
> For the generally received distinction between poetry and verse, he said in *For My Contemporaries,* derives from a widely and deeply felt discrimination not merely between the products of writing but also between the attitudes with which the act of writing is approached and between the kinds of life which surround and supplement it. Verse is a professional activity, social and objective, and its methods and standards are those of craftsmanship. It is a concern of the ordinary human self, and is on the whole within a man's power to do well or not. Its virtues are the civic virtues. If it lacks much, what it does have is ascertainable and can be judged. But poetry is amateurish, religious, and eminently unsociable. It dwells in the spiritual life, in the private haunts of theology or voodoo. It is passive to the powers it cannot evoke. It is the accidental issue, the plain bastard, of grace and inspiration, or of the demons of anxiety—even of somatic irritation, for indigestion may be your angel. In that region the elected of God and the elected of themselves are scarcely distinguishable, and if the true oracle is nonsense to sense, so nonsense is often taken for oracle. (*CE,* 406)

EPIGRAMS

An Epitaph for Anyone

Written in Los Altos in summer 1940.

The Scarecrow

Written in Stanford in spring 1934. Cunningham came to associate (*CE*, 416) this poem with the later "Autumn." Both depict scenes or objects that represent a forswearing of romantic adventure.

With a Detective Story

Written in Los Altos in December 1940.

8 By Aristotle's saws brings crimes to light: Many have noted (e.g., Dorothy L. Sayers, "Aristotle on Detective Fiction," in her *Unpopular Opinions* [New York: Harcourt Brace, 1947]) that the description of tragedy that Aristotle gives in his *Poetics* is applicable to the detective story. Both genres aim for exciting reversals and dramatic recognitions, and both seek to surprise the audience without violating its sense of plausibility and probability. Readers of detective stories often try to figure out, as they read, whodunit. A scholar would naturally use Aristotelian maxims as a guide. For many years, Cunningham himself read mysteries recreationally.

"Jove courted Danaë"

Written in Palo Alto in winter 1935. For the story of Jove (Zeus) and Danaë, see note above to "All Choice Is Error."

The Lover's Ghost Returns to the Underworld

Written in Los Altos in June 1941. This epigram adapts Propertius, *Elegies*, 4.7.91–94:

> *luce iubent leges Lethaea ad stagna reverti:*
> *nos vehimur, vectum nauta recenset onus.*
> *nunc te possideant aliae: mox sola tenebo:*
> *mecum eris, et mixtis ossibus ossa teram.*

At daylight the law orders us to return to Lethe's waters: we board, the boatman who conveys us counts his freight. Now others possess you: soon only I shall hold you: you will be mine, and we'll press bone against mingled bone.

In Propertius's elegy, these lines are spoken to the poet by Cynthia's ghost.

"Homer was poor"

Written in Los Altos in September 1941.

1-2 Homer was poor . . . as many Homers as you please: In the Classical Age Homer was believed to have been a blind bard who made his living by wandering from city to city and reciting his poems. However, some modern scholars have doubted that Homer existed and have suggested that the two epics attributed to him were amalgamated, over generations, from songs and poems by various poets. Friedrich August Wolf's *Prolegomena to Homer* (1795) focused this so-called "Homeric Question." A chief activity of this "Analytic" (as opposed to "Unitarian") approach has been to try to identify the different hands or Homers responsible for the different parts of the epics. For various reasons, current scholarship has edged back toward the opinion that one author is responsible for *The Iliad* (though he may have drawn on earlier material) and that one and perhaps the same author is responsible for *The Odyssey*. It is, though, unlikely that the issue will ever be settled, and the situation that Cunningham's epigram addresses will probably continue.

"Time heals not"

Written in Los Altos in October 1941.

August Hail

Written in Los Altos in September 1941. Of this poem, Cunningham says:

> Its subject was the sudden incidence of passion, which comes like an impersonal force and apparently from the outside; and it had a moral: "Who shall revenge unreason?" though it destroy all. The meter of the poem was accentual: four, three, four, and two accents a line. (*CE,* 415)

Montana Pastoral

Written in Los Altos in September 1941. Cunningham describes this as

> a curt autobiography . . . in which the details of fear, thirst, hunger, and the desperation of this huddled chill were hardly a just summary of his first twenty years but rather an epigrammatic presentation of the salient motives those years communicated to his later life. (*CE,* 418)

Cunningham reports that most of the poem's details derive from summers that he spent as a boy on a dry-land ranch "thirty-six miles from Billings, over the rimrock in the Wheat Basin country" (Steele, "Interview with J. V. Cunningham," 3). The ranch was owned by one of Cunningham's father's friends. However, Cunningham adds that the "huddled chill" comes from a later experience. In late fall or early winter of 1930, when he and his brother were driving south from Denver to Santa Fe, they "ran into a sudden blizzard and stayed for some days at a little cabin just short of the top of Raton Pass, just north of the New Mexico border" (ibid., 9). For a fine discussion of this poem, see Shankman, *In Search of the Classic*, 205–13.

This Tower of Sun

Written in Los Altos in September 1941. Entitled, in *TH* and *ER*, "Unromantic Love." Cunningham writes of this poem:

> In *This Tower of Sun* he represented a decision on the alternatives suggested by the incidence of passion. The romantic experience of stillness and light, occurring in some solitary natural surrounding, with its quasi-mystical intimation of a vague absolute . . . is an illusory experience. . . . The experience of romantic love is analogous, and its phantom object is contrived as willfully as the romantic object of such quasi-mystical experiences. But only a realized particular embodies the concept of love, the true ideal. What might be conjectured from such an experience as this—a romantic, higher, unrealized love—is precisely the absence of the Absolute; it is the undifferentiated many, realizable in no particular one, for if realized it would no longer have its characteristic property of being unspecific. (*CE*, 415; 416)

Like the more accessible "Metaphysical Amorist," this poem seems implicitly to reject the negative view of haecceity that Cunningham expresses in such poems as "Haecceity" and "Agnosco Veteris Vestigia Flammae" and in such prose statements as "The more realized a thing is the greater its defect of being" (*CE*, 412). That is, in "This Tower of Sun" Cunningham proposes that the realized particular and the abstract ideal are fused. Though "Thisness" is not identical with ideality, it is inseparable from it—and vice versa.

Autumn

Written in Los Altos in September 1941. Cunningham writes that this poem represented an admission of the failure of the quest of the opal—the quest for romantic and aesthetic fulfillment. It was a poem in which the whole manner of the quest was devoted to acquiescence in what amounted to its abandonment. Here experience has ripened for the harvest, the time of falling leaves, the time of acceptance—even of indifference—when grief is subdued to the resignation of the season. . . . This is, if you will, a manifestation of tiredness of spirit, an embracing of fatigue. And so you may object that no sound moralist should retire and live sufficient to himself, seeking, as it were, a cloistered virtue. He answered that this is but the necessary act of the man of experience, the tried. He cannot keep the occasions of adventure or of hope far *from* his heart . . . but he may and will keep them hidden far *in* his heart. He is acquainted with the occasions of adventure whose symbol is the passing train, but he will not heed their persuasions for he knows there is in them no abiding rest. (*CE,* 416)

Reason and Nature

Written in Los Altos in September 1941. The poem involves an assertion of the simultaneous reality of not only reason and nature, but also ideality and sensation. We can view, Cunningham suggests, our experience or identity abstractly and can judge neatly from the outside. Yet at the same time we are our experience and are inextricably involved in its immediate and changing processes and confusions. (The "Reason" in the poem's title is associated with the ideal or detached view of experience and identity; "Nature" is associated with the messy-taffy actualities of experience and identity.) Cunningham's gloss on the poem is almost as thorny as the poem itself, but his general drift is clear:

The pool in a pure frame is the projection of reason in which reason can only see its own construction, and one's notion of his identity is such a construction. The unchanging, unalterable pool, therefore, is a fiction, a device of method. But what we call the real pool, the pool of sensation and experience where we may find a willow or two, is not unrippled. Though the alterations in its surface be as minute as the slight waves caused by skimming flies, these results of chaos and change will exemplify no given rule, will be the realization of no definable method. . . .

In brief, he characterized [in stanza one] the Idealist as one whose Ideals reflect merely their postulation. He now characterized [in stanza three] the Sensationalist as a Narcissus who cannot possibly see his identity on the irrational surface of experience. . . .

He asserted that he was both Sensationalist and Idealist, both change and constancy, both material and method. He knew both what he saw and what he thought, confusion and clarity, and though these were distinct and separate the one was applicable to the other, method to material, and applicable only because they were distinct. . . . A man is distinct from his experience or he could not speak of it, yet he is his experience or it would not be his. He must be both disinterested and engrossed. (*CE*, 422–23)

L'Esprit de Géométrie et L'Esprit de Finesse

Written in Los Altos in September 1941. The title is borrowed from Pascal's *Pensées*. It heads that section of the *Pensées* in which Pascal contrasts the mathematical mind *(l'esprit de géométrie)* with the intuitive mind *(l'esprit de finesse)*. The epigraph from Pascal comes from a different section of the *Pensées* devoted to Imagination—Imagination considered not as the aesthetic and productive faculty, but rather as that superstitious faculty that can override the rational capacities of even the most intelligent people. Pascal asks rhetorically, "Who does not know that the sight of cats, of rats, the collapse of an ember, etc., can rip reason off its hinges?" The epigraph from Saint Bonaventure runs, "The human soul is ruled by a violence of reason." In the poem, Cunningham seems to say that we can get fixated either by the rational mind or by the superstitious spirit. The Bonaventure epigraph suggests the process of getting unhinged ("Distraught") by the rational mind ("thought"); the Pascal epigraph suggests the process of getting unhinged by the superstitious spirit ("sense"). It is probably beside the point that Cunningham appears to connect, in an unPascalian manner, *l'esprit de finesse* with the merely superstitious and sensory. (For Pascal both the mathematical spirit and the intuitive spirit are intellectually valuable and opposed to the kinds of spooked responses that the sight of rats or collapsing embers may produce.) Cunningham remarks of this poem: "He said (in *L'Esprit*): So far as I am—and perhaps it is a matter of temperament—I am the idea that informs my experience; it is the Idea by whose evil eye I am held as men were by the legendary basilisk" (*CE*, 421). Cunningham's implication is that he responds to impersonal conceptions—the domain of the mathematical mind—in a visceral way customarily associated with the intuitive spirit.

6 Pascal: Blaise Pascal (1623–1662) was a French philosopher, theologian, and scientist. **Bonaventure** (1221–1274) was a Franciscan theologian and philosopher.

Bookplate

Written in Stanford in November 1933.

The Judge Is Fury (1942)

Epigraph to The Judge Is Fury

Written in Palo Alto on March 3, 1944.

The Phoenix

Begun at Stanford in December 1933 and completed in Honolulu in 1946. Cunningham mentioned in conversation that the poem was largely written at the earlier date, and he included this poem in the 1931–1934 section of *CPE*. The phoenix is a legendary bird reputed to live in the Arabian desert. Every five hundred years it dies and is born again from its ashes. Early Christians regarded the phoenix as a symbol of the resurrection, though the speaker of this poem seems unconvinced by the doctrine of immortality ("I have not found you . . . I have not found you . . . Though I am told that I shall find you"). The poem's stanzas feature not only cross rhyme in the first four lines: internal rhyme links the middles of the fourth lines with the ends of fifth (varying/burying, told/cold, singing/flinging). John Baxter has observed ("The Province of the Plain Style," 34) that these semi-concealed internal rhymes suggest the simultaneous presence and non-presence of the bird, and the speaker's simultaneous skepticism and desire to believe.

    2 Nor . . . nor: A once common but now increasingly archaic form for "Neither . . . nor." This construction—and the related "Or . . . or . . ." for "Either . . . or . . ."—derive from analogous constructions in Latin and French. In Latin, "neither . . . nor" and "either . . . or" are rendered, respectively, *nec . . . nec* and *aut . . . aut*. In French, *ni . . . ni* and *ou . . . ou* are used.

In Innocence

Written in Denver in August 1931. In his copy of *CPE,* Cunningham attaches two plus signs to the date, evidently to indicate that the poem was revised after its initial composition or publication. When the poem first appeared in *The Commonweal* (February 10, 1932), it was entitled "Retreating Friendship," and ran, without stanza division,

> In earlier day we said:
> Affection is secure;
> It is not forced or led.

No longer sure
Of hallowed certainty
I have erased the mind,
As mendicants that see
Mimic the blind.

When Cunningham re-published the poem in *YSW* 3 (June 1932), he altered the opening line to "Our testament had read," changed "that" in line 7 to "who," and added the stanza division. The poem appeared in its current form in *JF* and *ER,* though in these two collections it was entitled "Experience."

Noon

Written in Denver in August 1931. In his copy of *CPE,* Cunningham attaches a plus sign to the date, evidently to indicate that the poem was revised thereafter. When first published in *YSW* 3 (June 1932), the poem was entitled "Hymn for the Sixth Hour," had an additional stanza, and was otherwise different from its final version:

From the unshriven sun we hoard
Studied release,
Soft as the city unheard
While noon bells ring nor peace

Nor disquiet: the self's own stir,
Autonomous,
Alone, as on the stair
At time of angelus,

Halting, the worshippers repeat
An exorcism;
The angled clock's repute
Conjured with chrism.

Whether in its earlier or later version, the poem is difficult. Cunningham never commented, or at least not in print, on the poem.

4 Angelus: A devotion or exercise of the Roman Catholic Church that commemorates the Annunciation. It is observed at morning, noon, and evening, and is named after the first word of the service: *Angelus domini nuntiavit Mariae* ("An angel of God announced to Mary"). **7 repute:** Evidently the word is used in the sense of the Latin *reputare,* "to compute." The clock, that is, is striking twelve and counting the hours. **8 chrism:** "Oil mingled with balm, consecrated for use as an unguent in the administration of certain sacraments in the Eastern and Western Churches" *(OED)*.

Distinctions at Dusk

Written in Palo Alto in January 1932. Cunningham glosses the poem thus:

> Reason is light which distinguishes reality into shapes and shadows, but there are times and conditions in which all is shaded or light so diffused that nothing is distinguishable. Such are the obscure regions of spiritual pride where the sharp edge of reason cannot penetrate, yet such regions can in their own terms and by their own methods be mapped and charted. *(CE,* 410)

The same interest in "times and conditions in which . . . nothing is distinguishable" appears in "Coffee" (see note below on that poem).

Ripeness Is All

Written at Stanford in November 1933. The title comes from *King Lear* 5.2.9–11. Lear and his allies have been temporarily routed, and Edgar is urging a despairing Gloucester not to give up and die before his time, but to bestir himself and join in the general retreat from Edmund's forces:

> Men must endure
> Their going hence even as their coming hither:
> Ripeness is all.

Cunningham analyzes the phrase (though not his use of it for this poem) in *Woe or Wonder,* his study of Shakespeare's tragedies.

The Chase

Written in Denver in spring 1934. In his copy of *CPE,* Cunningham attaches a plus sign to the date, indicating that the poem was revised thereafter. When the poem first appeared, in *The New Republic* 80 (November 7, 1934), it began:

> The wind swelling the eyes with tears
> Moves slower than the startled doe.
> Tailored and white, the rabbit veers
> As if she had a whim to go.
>
> Running she crossed and dodged and turned; . . .

Cunningham subsequently cut the opening stanza, so as to begin with what had been line five, altering it to "The rabbit crossed and dodged and turned." He made a few other changes in the body of the poem. He once said of this poem that it "is a beast fable" (Cunningham, notes on Yvor Winters, "The Poetry of J.V. Cunningham," Sudbury, Mass.: June 6, 1967; unpublished notes, 2).

9 Kaw: *Webster's New Geographical Dictionary* (Springfield, Mass.: Merriam-Webster, 1988) reports that this is another name for the Kansas river, which, "formed by confluence of Republican and Smoky Hill rivers at Junction City, Geary co., E. Kansas, flows E into Missouri river at Kansas City." Cunningham would have known the river and the area through which it flows from his semester at St. Mary's College in Kansas.

Coffee

Written in Palo Alto in fall 1935. In his copy of *CPE,* Cunningham attaches a plus sign to the date, evidently to indicate that the poem was revised thereafter. In "Quest of the Opal," Cunningham associates this poem with the earlier "Distinction at Dusk." Both deal with

> the same area of engrossing irrational experience, one that did not respect the distinction between subjective and objective ("That no glass can oppose"). . . . You cannot take these [experiences] by the throat and throttle them, for there is nothing to get your hands on; you must outwait and outwit them; you must distract yourself and them by some odd device or other. Yet there were values there, curious accessions of insight and energy, intimations beyond the routine, and an ordering of all by an adjustment to the consistent grayness of a mood. But there was also waste and the perception of waste. (*CE,* 410)

When the poem was initially published in *Twelve Poets of the Pacific,* ed. Yvor Winters (Norfolk, Conn.: New Directions, 1937), it was entitled "Dusk," had an additional stanza, and concluded

> . . . In an uncumbered clime
> Minute inductions wake.
>
> And I waste time because
> When private panics seize
> The soul and twilight draws
> Us anywhere you please,
>
> One wastes it for the waste.
> I wonder who's to blame.

Can we live so, ungraced?
Can we go on the same?

18 nor . . . nor: About this construction, see the note to "The Phoenix."

To a Friend, on Her Examination for the Doctorate in English

Written in Palo Alto in spring 1936. In his copy of *CPE,* Cunningham attaches a plus sign to the date, evidently to indicate that the poem was revised thereafter. When this poem first appeared in *Twelve Poets of the Pacific,* it was entitled "To Miss Evelyn C. Johnson (On Her Examination for the Doctorate in English, Stanford University, 1936)." For the final version of the poem, Cunningham made a number of small revisions, as well as deleting a couplet about ". . . the words of men / Whom few will ever read again."

14 Tudor: A reference to the royal house of Tudor, the family that ruled England from 1485 to 1603. Ms. Johnson was apparently, like Cunningham, a student of Renaissance literature.

Passion

Written in Los Altos in September 1941. Of this poem, Cunningham says:

> He wrote . . . *(Passion)* in which he developed a pun on the word, on passion in the ordinary sense as an aspect of love and passion as the philosophic complement of act. The pun is taken as implying reality. Passion in the ordinary sense is here said to involve all that is unrealized in any particular act of love. By definition, then, it is unrealizable in terms of act. But in its own terms, as involving all the potentialities of love, surmised or rejected, it is latent in each act, surrounds it and gives resonance to it. The act is the tone of which passion is all the overtones. By this device he found a place for all those possible experiences that haunted his appetite and for which circumstance or morality afforded no actual place. *(CE, 415)*

The Metaphysical Amorist

Written in Los Altos in spring 1940. In his copy of *CPE,* Cunningham attaches a plus sign to the date, evidently to indicate that the poem was revised thereafter. When it first appeared in *New Mexico Quarterly Review* 12 (August 1942), this poem had a seven-line preamble that Cunningham subsequently cut. Of this poem, Cunningham writes:

He . . . dealt with the problem of universals in *The Metaphysical Amorist* [which involved] . . . the idea of Love and the situation one finds himself in. These are separate and distinct orders of reality, and yet relatable to each other, as the man who sees is distinct from what he sees and yet his way of seeing determines what it is he sees. (*CE,* 422)

Here as elsewhere, Cunningham urges that different views of an issue may be equally and simultaneously valid. In this case, Cunningham suggests that we can experience Love in its timeless and transcendent aspect, at the same time that we experience its immediate presence in an individual whom we love. As Cunningham puts it, "I know her in both ways [transcendently and particularly] at once." As with "This Tower of Sun," this poem suggests that things are metaphysically real in both their universality and their haecceity—their "thisness."

27–31 Plato . . . Duns: Plato (c. 428–347 B.C.) urged that reality ultimately resides in Forms or Ideas. God creates these, and we can apprehend them only through thought, not sense. David Hume (1711–1776), in contrast, denied the ulitmate reality of Forms or Ideas, suggesting that they are just extrapolations from or compounds of sense impressions. John Duns Scotus (c. 1266–1308) urged, as is noted in the introduction to this volume, a dual position. Things express universal Form *and* particular Individuation, and these two qualities are inseparable in their existential manifestations.

Envoi

Written in Palo Alto on February 2, 1942.

Not for Charity

Written in Balboa, California, in November 1942. In *JF* and *ER,* this poem is entitled "Forgiveness."

The Predestined Space

Begun in Balboa in November 1942 and completed (or revised) in Honolulu in 1946. In *JF* and *ER* this poem was entitled "Apology." When it initially appeared in *New Mexico Quarterly Review* 13 (Autumn 1943), the poem was entitled "Commendatory Verses for a Friend's Book" and ran

> Good faith gives simple lines,
> Or, rather, uncomplex,

Which wariness refines
And doubts perplex

Until the engineer
Of metre, rhyme, and thought
Can only tool each gear
To what he sought

If chance with craft combines
In the predestined space
To lend his damaged lines
Redeeming grace.

So is it in these pages.
By grace the damaged heart
(Once in how seldom ages!)
Issues in art.

For the final version of the poem, Cunningham dropped the first stanza and substituted in its place a rewritten last stanza; and by introducing the first-person pronoun ("So would I in these pages / If will were art"), he made the poem apply to himself and to writing generally rather than to the particular book of the person originally addressed. The poem, then, began as a treatment of one subject, but revealed itself to have a different and more comprehensive concern. When Cunningham recognized this (and an ability to make such recognitions is a key trait of good poets), he recast the poem accordingly.

Acknowledgement

According to Gullans's *Bibliography* and working copy of *CPE,* this poem was, like "The Predestined Space," begun in Balboa in November 1942 and completed in Honolulu in 1946. Cunningham simply notes, in his copy of *CPE,* "Nov. '42 | Balboa." A version of the poem slightly different from the final one appeared in *New Mexico Quarterly Review* 13 (August 1943). Perhaps the second date in Gullans refers to the time that the poem was revised into its final form. In *JF* and *ER* the poem was entitled "On a Nice Book."

Ars Amoris

Written in Balboa in March 1943. The title is Latin for "The Art of Love" and alludes to the titles of Ovid's verse treatises about love and lovers—the *Amores,* the *Ars Amatoria,* and the *Remedia Amoris.*

Haecceity

Written in Balboa in June 1943. For discussion of Cunningham's interest in haecceity, see the introduction to this book, as well as the notes to "All Choice Is Error," "This Tower of Sun," "The Metaphysical Amorist," "Agnosco Veteris Vestigia Flammae," and "How We Desire Desire."

Convalescence

Written in Balboa on February 12, 1943.

To My Daimon

No place or date of composition in Gullans, but Cunningham notes in his copy of *CPE,* "Dec. '43, + | Palo Alto"—the plus sign evidently indicating, here as elsewhere, that Cunningham revised the poem after initially completing it. When the poem first appeared in *New Mexico Quarterly Review* 14 (Summer 1944), the fifth and final couplet read not "Who know myself within / The sinner and the sin," but rather "Self-knower, self-aware, / Self-knowledge is despair."

8 Daimon: "[A] direct transliteration of Gr. *daimōn* divinity, one's genius or DEMON" (*OED*). As this definition suggests, the word has carried, from the Greeks to our time, a negative as well as a neutral connotation. One's daimon may be understood as one's guiding spirit, but it may also be conceived of as one's evil genius or fate.

The Man of Feeling

Written in Palo Alto in September 1943.

8 Pythagoras and Protagoras: Ancient philosophers who represent opposing points of view. Pythagoras (c. 582–c. 500 B.C.) argued that the universe is governed by number. He is associated with the belief in the "harmony of spheres," and he discovered, among other things, the mathematical foundation of musical intervals. In the Pythagorean view, knowledge and judgment can attain objective validity, at least so far as they are based on mathematical calculation. Protagoras (c. 481–c. 411 B.C.), in contrast, holds a relativistic position. According to his well-known maxim (Plato, *Theaetetus,* 160D), "Man is the measure of all things." Judgment, by this formula, is subjective, and science can claim no transcendent validity. Cunningham's description of the man of feeling is critical. Someone who can fuse Pythagoras and Protagoras is probably ignoring or simplifying difficult intellectual and emotional questions. This interpretation is supported by the fact that Cunningham always placed this poem, from the time of its first book appearance in *JF,* next to "The Solipsist."

The Solipsist

Begun in Palo Alto in 1943 and completed there in February 1944. Cunningham places in his copy of *CPE* a plus sign after the second date, evidently to indicate that he later revised the poem. Such revision must have occurred before the poem was first published in *JR:* other than having a few variants in the punctuation, the printings of the poem over the years do not differ from one another.

Agnosco Veteris Vestigia Flammae

Begun in Palo Alto in September of 1943 and completed in the same place in January 1944. The title comes from *Aeneid* 4.23. Dido, having pledged fidelity to the memory of her murdered husband Sychaeus, nevertheless feels herself falling in love with Aeneas and tells her sister, "I recognize the traces of the old flame [of love]." As with several other of Cunningham's poems, this one expresses the idea that particular choices and attachments result in a diminution of being. The poem concerns as well the plain human fact that falling in love can be a frightening experience, in which one feels helpless and disoriented. Section XI of "The Journal of John Cardan" paraphrases the poem:

> One recognizes with the misgivings of experience the imminence of the state of passion, of engrossed choice of an object to love. But the state of passion is an emanation of the indeterminable sources of personal identity, the void region of possibilities where dwells the promise of multiple and unrestricted fulfillments. The realm of history, personal or public, where particular acts occur in particular times and places is something else again. Hence love, the allegiance of passion to a given external object, betrays this inner void whose principle of being is to be neither this nor that, to be pregnant with every possible future, because not committed to any particular one. But choice turns the unconditioned idea into a conditioned process, into a succession of acts whose ultimate intention gives structure to each as it happens, while the feeling that surrounds each act hurries it on to its successor. So intimation falls away into fact. (*CE,* 429)

Distraction

Written in Palo Alto on March 3, 1944.

Meditation on Statistical Method

Written in Balboa in May 1943. Winters (*Forms of Discovery*, 304) says of the poem:

> The opening lines contrast Plato's theory of numbers as absolute forms with a modern theory of numbers as statistical and relativistic devices; but this contrast is merely the vehicle—the poem deals with theories of the understanding of human experience. In the tenth line we have the word *hyperbole*, the name of a figure of speech, exaggeration. But the word *hyperbola* is the name of a mathematical curve which never returns to intersect itself. One can call this a pun in the grand manner of the Renaissance or a condensed metaphor, as one prefers. The poem is witty in the best sense, but it is more than that: it is a statement about the irreducibility of human passion.

14 Nor . . . nor: About this construction, see remarks in the note to "The Phoenix."

Meditation on a Memoir

Written in Palo Alto on August 21, 1943.

To the Reader

Written in Palo Alto on July 14, 1943.

Epigrams: A Journal

"Each that I loved"

Written in Honolulu on May 17, 1946. Cunningham evidently composed this epigram as preface for "The Journal of Epigrams" that he was gathering together for and that would appear the following year in *JE*. The epigram is the last one of "The Journal" to have been written, with the apparent exception of "A Is A: Monism Refuted." (Though this latter epigram bears the date of "Spring 1946" and could thus be earlier than "May 17," Gullans lists the epigram immediately after "Each that I loved"; and in the mostly chronological epigram section of *CPE,* Cunningham places "A Is A" after "Each that I loved.")

2 severally: Separately. In other words, though once close to those addressed, the poet now "exists apart" from them.

"I don't know what I am "

Written in Santa Barbara in August 1941. "On a Line from Bodenham's 'Belvedere'" is a later epigram that treats the same theme, which is also examined from a different perspective in "Meditation on a Memoir."

"If I can't know myself"

Written in Palo Alto in August 1945.

"Give not yourself to apology"

Written in Stanford in fall 1933. This is the earliest epigram that Cunningham collected in a book. Though he printed it in *JF* and *ER*, he dropped it from *CPE*.

With a Book of Clavier Music

Written in Palo Alto in 1935. Though "Clavier" has several meanings, it suggests mainly a pre-piano keyboard instrument such as a harpsichord; and Cunningham may in this epigram be referring to Baroque musical scores in which harmonic elements are implied rather than written out. As one authority puts it:

> The most characteristic texture of the Baroque period was not imitative counterpoint . . . but rather a texture that emphasized the two outer voices—the melody and bass—held together by "filler" harmonies. In about 1600 the preference for this texture led to the rise of a musical shorthand known as *basso continuo* or *thoroughbass,* in which the composer wrote out only the melody and bass in full and simply indicated the desired harmonies by numerals or accidentals place above or below the bass part (a practice known as *figured bass).* One or more performers playing instruments capable of producing harmony (e.g., the harpsichord, organ or lute) improvised (or *realized)* the harmonies implied by the figured bass, while another performer reinforced the bass line on a sustaining melodic instrument such as a violoncello or bassoon. The use of the basso continuo throughout the period was such an important feature of the Baroque style that some historians have referred to the period itself as the "thoroughbass period" (Entry for "Basso Continuo" in Hugh M. Miller, Paul Taylor, and Edgar W. Williams, *Introduction to Music,* 3rd ed. [New York: HarperCollins, 1991]).

If Cunningham has in mind this Baroque practice, "unthought," "unclear," and "error" refer to the music's being incompletely indicated in the score; and the "human hand" is the composer's. However, Cunningham may mean the adjectives "unthought" and "unclear" to indicate that music, though having a "planned" structure, is not limited by specifically articulated ideas or material contents. If this interpretation is correct, then "error" is a synonym for "mistake"; and the "human hand" is that of a performer who fails to render a musical score (unerring in its conception or "nature") as its composer wrote it. Cunningham may also be referring to the idea that music "plans" (in the sense of "arranges" rather than "intends") inchoate impressions and wandering reveries.

"My dear, though I have left no sigh"

Written in Palo Alto in 1934. Cunningham wrote this epigram for his mother after her death; when the poem initially appeared in 1937 in *Twelve Poets of the Pacific,* the first line read, "Mother, though I leave no sad sigh." Though Cunningham collected this epigram in both *JF* and *ER,* he dropped it from *CPE.*

3 name, and: Though I have not tinkered elsewhere with Cunningham's punctuation, I have added a comma here, so as to avoid the possible reading of "Your name and your flesh" as a pair of direct objects rather than as a direct object and a subject of a new clause, respectively. (Cunningham did not relish grammatical ambiguities, and it is unlikely that he intended to create one in this epigram.)

"All hastens to its end"

Written in Santa Barbara in August 1941. This epigram varies one by John Owen (1563?–1622). According to the standard edition of Owen's ten books of epigrams, this is 1.36—the thirty-sixth poem from the first book:

De Vita et Venere

Omnis ad extremum properet licet actio finem;
Oderunt finem vita, Venusque suum.

Of Life and Love

Although all activity hurries to its conclusion, life and love hate their end.

"If wisdom, as it seems it is"

Written in Santa Barbara on September 1, 1941.

"Within this mindless vault"

Written in Palo Alto in summer 1942.

2 Tristan and Isolt: One of the most popular stories of medieval literature was that of Tristan and Isolt. Variously told by different writers in different languages, it involves essentially the following: King Mark of Cornwall sends his knight and nephew Tristan to Ireland to bring the beautiful princess Isolt to the Cornish court to marry the king. Isolt's mother prepares a love philter to be drunk by King Mark and Isolt to bind them together in deep and everlasting affection. By accident Tristan and Isolt drink the potion. They fall in love and become rapturously indifferent to anything except their sexual joy in one another. Thanks to chance and discreditable dodges, they manage to continue their affair for a time before and after Isolt's marriage to Mark. However, they are ultimately discovered, and everybody comes to a miserable end.

"Grief restrains grief"

Written in Palo Alto in summer of 1942, according to Gullans, and September 1942, according to Cunningham in his copy of *CPE*.

"When I shall be without regret"

Written in Palo Alto in summer 1942. Twenty years later Paul Engle and Joseph Langland asked a number of American poets to pick for an anthology a favorite poem that they themselves had written and to state the reasons for their choice; Cunningham selected this epigram and said of it: "I like this poem because it is all denotation and no connotation; because it has only one level of meaning; because it is not ironic, paradoxical, complex, or subtle; and because the meter is monotonously regular" (Paul Engle and Joseph Langland, eds., *Poet's Choice* [New York: Dial Press, 1962], 105).

"I was concerned for you "

Written in Palo Alto in August 1942.

On the Cover of My First Book

Written in Palo Alto on March 11, 1942. Cunningham's first collection of poems, *The Helmsman,* was published in January 1942 in an edition of 300 copies by Jane Grabhorn's Colt Press. The book is beautiful, but it was not what Cunningham had expected. Gullans describes the book and cover:

> Bound in cream colored wall paper with a flower pattern in magenta and cerise over boards, the top and bottom edges yapped; endpapers, sewn. On the front cover there is a label, 3 15/16" x 2 1/2", of pale gray, blue or white paper, printed in red within a double border of rules and ornaments, "The Helmsman | by J.V. Cunningham | [in black letter] Colt Press Poetry Booklets: Number 2." (*Bibliography*, 1)

Gullans adds: "At Cunningham's insistence (see *On the Cover of My First Book*) some copies were bound in a neutral dark, grayish-green paper over boards with various labels." There is a chapter on the fine-press work of the Grabhorns—Edwin, Robert, and Jane (Edwin and Robert were brothers, and Jane was Robert's wife)—in Joseph Blumenthal, *The Printed Book in America* (Boston: Godine, 1977), 117–23.

3–4 flowery dress . . . wild wallpaper: As Gullans's description indicates, the dust jacket of the book was, literally, made of wallpaper, with a floral design.

"*What is this visage?*"

Written in Palo Alto on March 13, 1942, shortly after the publication of *The Helmsman*. The "ghost" in this epigram is the ghost of the romantic quest described and ultimately abandoned in that book. Of the epigram, Cunningham writes:

> On the publication of his book he revived that final crisis in memory, and recorded the vision in an epigram. . . . It was a ghost he had laid and, as a man will, had conjured again, whose values were an envisaged, though rejected, way of life, still happily unstayed by the voice of desire, still escaping though called, and escaping because dismayed by the intrinsic fears for which it had been previously rejected. The ghost was not the person—no ghost is—but the experience the person evoked: the temptation to the continued pursuit of the quest. (*CE*, 417)

"*Deep summer, and time pauses*"

In his copy of *CPE*, Cunningham records the place and date of composition as "Oct. '41 Los Altos." Gullans gives "Palo Alto, February 4, 1942." This latter listing is also that of the following epigram. Possibly when Gullans was assembling his *Bibliography* there was a miscommunication between him and Cunningham regarding where and when "Deep Summer" was written, with the result it acquired the data for the neighboring epigram.

"The dry soul rages"

Written in Palo Alto on February 4, 1942.

"Dear, if unsocial privacies obsess me"

Written, according to Cunningham's copy of *CPE,* in Palo Alto on October 30, 1943. (Gullans lists October 3 of the same year as the date; possibly, the zero fell out of his date at some point in his work.)

"Deep sowing of our shame"

Written in Santa Barbara on August 30, 1941.

"In this child's game"

Written in Balboa in December 1942.

"After some years Bohemian came to this"

Written in Balboa in spring 1943. (In his copy of *CPE,* Cunningham attaches a plus sign to the date, evidently to indicate that the poem was revised thereafter.)

"Genius is born and made"

Written in Balboa in spring 1943. In connection with this epigram, Cunningham once described the process by which he wrote many of his poems:

> I often find that I have odd lines here and there that suggest something, and, of course, much that I write is suggested by a phrase in language, and then I find a kind of meaning that this phrase could assume. For instance, there's a little epigram which reads:
>
> > Genius is born and made. This heel who mastered
> > By infinite pains his trade was born a bastard.

I recall the genesis of that. I was sitting over coffee, just toying with the idea of finding a good rhyme for "bastard." Then I thought of "mastered," and then I thought of mastering an art. Then I thought of genius—is it born or made?—and of genius as the capacity for taking infinite pains. In brief, all these, so to speak, fossils in the language entered into it. When I had finished, I could think of a number of real situations, real persons, to whom it would refer. (Steele, "Interview with J.V. Cunningham," 23–24)

"I showed some devils"

Written in Balboa in March 1943. Though Cunningham collected this epigram in both *JF* and *ER,* he dropped it from *CPE.*

2 Freudian: Sigmund Freud (1856–1939) founded psychoanalysis. His theories were and remain the subject of controversy. As this and several other poems indicate, Cunningham was skeptical of Freudianism. While Cunningham believed profoundly in the power of the irrational, he doubted that the evocation of buried fears and desires could, as Freud hoped, allay those forces. Cunningham, moreover, objected to Freud's use of traditional myth (see "An Oedipean Mom and Dad") and felt that aspects of Freudian thought were more matters of faith than of science (see "The True Religion"). Additional poems or epigrams by Cunningham that refer to psychoanalysis include "Interview with Doctor Drink" and "The Elders at Their Services."

"Dark thoughts are my companions"

Written in Balboa in March 1943.

"Action is memoir"

Written in Palo Alto on September 29, 1943. In his "Journal of John Cardan," Cunningham makes comments that could serve as a paraphrase for this epigram:

I have been reflecting on the common notions about intellectualism. I have observed that the intellectual, unless it be a fraud, derives its content and its vitality from emotion and experience. An intellectual distinction is both an emotional experience in itself, in the perception of it, and a realignment of the emotional experiences which are the content of the distinction. Hence the history of a man's thought is memoir as well as the history of his emotional life. (*CE,* 427–28)

Cunningham suggests here that we can infer a writer's emotional life from his or her thought. The writer does not necessarily need to present steamy details—"scandal"—to convey emotional history. Cunningham's comment also suggests that the epigram might just as well have opened, "Thought is memoir" or "One's thought is memoir." ("Action" perhaps causes a small confusion, since the connection being made is not really between action and memoir, but between thought and memoir.) However, Cunningham uses "thought" in the second line; had he used it in the first as well, the epigram might have sounded awkwardly repetitive. In any case, the main point is that memoir can be something—such as action or thought—other than emotion and scandal.

Motto for a Sun Dial

Written in Balboa in October 1942. Epigrams about sun dials comprise a virtual sub-genre of the form. Among modern epigrammatists, Hilaire Belloc (1870–1953) has written humorous epigrams about the instrument, one of which goes,

> I am a sun dial, and I make a botch
> Of what is done much better by a watch.

History of Ideas

Written in Balboa in spring 1943.

1 God is love: The maxim comes from *The First Letter of John,* 4.8: "He who does not love does not know God; for God is love." **1–2 conversion:** The word is used, first, with its meaning in logic—the transposition of the subject and predicate of a proposition—and, second, with its meaning in religion—the process by which an unbeliever acquires faith or by which a person switches affiliation from one church to another. Winters comments on this epigram, "These lines give us a succinct summary of a major transition: they take us from the New Testament to W. B. Yeats" (*Forms of Discovery,* 307).

On the Calculus

Written in Balboa in October 1942, when Cunningham was teaching mathematics to pilots at the Seventh Army Air Base. If Cunningham refers to mathematics in exploring the idea that we moderns are dizzied by both the infinitely great and the infinitely small, Frost treats much the same theme in terms of the physical sciences, writing in "The Bear" (13–21),

Man acts more like the poor bear in a cage
That all day fights a nervous inward rage,
His mood rejecting all his mind suggests.
He paces back and forth and never rests
The toe-nail click and shuffle of his feet,
The telescope at one end of his beat,
And at the other end the microscope,
Two instruments of nearly equal hope
And in conjunction giving quite a spread. . . .

1 almost: Cunningham refers perhaps to the process in integral calculus of measuring things (e.g., areas enclosed within or under a curve) by a series of successively more accurate approximations. Or he may be thinking of certain sequential processes by which a limit is approached but never achieved, as in the formula,

$$\lim_{n \to \infty} {}^1\!/_n = 0$$

which indicates that the fraction $1/n$ approaches a limit of zero as n approaches infinity (∞). **3 Zero . . . limit . . . infinity:** The idea of limit is central to the calculus, and one of its haunting aspects is that its operations may simultaneously involve both the infinite and the infinitesimal. (Integral calculus and differential calculus are, considered together, sometimes termed "infinitesimal calculus.")

"Soft found a way"

Written in Palo Alto in 1944.

"Kiss me goodbye"

Written in Palo Alto on October 28, 1943.

2 uncloistered virtue: An allusion to John Milton's famous sentence in the *Areopagitica*: "I cannot praise a fugitive and cloistered virtue, unexercised and unbreathed, that never sallies out and sees her adversary, but slinks out of the race, where that immortal garland is to be run for, not without dust and heat."

"This Humanist"

Written in Palo Alto in 1944.

"He weeps and sleeps with Dido"

Like "Kiss Me Goodbye," written in Palo Alto on October 28, 1943.

1 Dido: The queen of Carthage who, in Virgil's *Aeneid*, shelters the wandering Aeneas and then kills herself when he abandons her. Modern readers have taken a severe view of Aeneas's desertion, though Jupiter (via Mercury) commands the Trojan to break off the affair and sail on to Italy and to his destiny; and the original Roman audience of the poem likely regarded Aeneas's departure as an act of self-sacrificing piety. Further, Dido is hardly the passive injured lover that some critics have imagined. She resolves to annihilate the Trojans before they leave Carthage (only thanks to a timely warning from Mercury do they escape), and she goes to her death with a barrage of curses on Aeneas and his descendants, curses whose fulfillment will bring about the Punic Wars.

"This is my curse. Pompous, I pray"

Written in Palo Alto in 1944.

"Silence is noisome"

Written in Balboa in spring 1943.

"How we desire desire"

Written in Palo Alto on October 1, 1943. Cunningham's paraphrase of this epigram runs:

> [T]he fundamental compulsion of one's life . . . is not love, lust, gregariousness, the will to live, or any of the emotions or instincts assigned to man. It is that to live is at every moment to be and to do some particularity: in this respect *what* does not matter, only it must be something. The void must be specified. Loneliness is an intimation of the void which we attempt to defeat by some more notable specification. Haecceity, or thisness, is the primal and ultimate compulsion of one's life; it is the principle of insufficient reason. (*CE,* 412)

"Hang up your weaponed wit"

Written in Palo Alto in August 1943.

"The self is terrified"

Written in Palo Alto on January 8, 1944.

"The scholar of theology and science"

Written in Palo Alto on January 5, 1944.

4–5 Love goes . . . merit: An allusion to longstanding debate in Christianity over whether people are saved by Grace (resulting from Faith) or by Works (indicative of self-acquired Merit).

"Dear, my familiar hand"

Written in Honolulu in fall 1945.

"Death in this music dwells"

Written in Balboa in spring 1943.

To a Student

Written in Palo Alto in fall 1943.

A Is A: Monism Refuted

Written in Honolulu in spring of 1946. Monism is a concept that has at different times taken on different meanings. (See the entries for "Anomalous Monism," "Monism and Pluralism," and "Neutral Monism" in Ted Honderich, ed., *The Oxford Companion to Philosophy* [Oxford: Oxford University Press, 1995]). Essentially, monism holds that reality has as its basis one substance or principle. Cunningham's epigram satirizes the reductive tendencies of monistic thought more than the philosophical concept itself. In the monism of Baruch Spinoza, for example, the universe is not emptied. Instead, Spinoza merely insists that one being or entity (God or Nature) fills the universe.

With a Copy of Swift's Works

Written in Palo Alto on May 20, 1944. Jonathan Swift (1667–1745) is the preeminent satirist in English literature. On Swift, see also the note for "The Wandering Scholar's Prayer to Saint Catherine of Egypt."

2 Vanessa's, Stella's lover: A reference to the two women who figured prominently in Swift's life. Esther Johnson (1681–1728) was the "Stella" to whom Swift wrote his memorable *Journal*. Swift met her when she was only eight years old, and his relations with her have been the subject of much conjecture. Some even speculate that they may have been secretly married in 1716; they did remain close until her death. "Vanessa" was Esther (also called "Hester") Vanhomrigh (1687? 1688?–1723), whom Swift met in 1708. Though twenty-one years his junior, she fell in love with him. Swift attempted to dissuade her from her affection, but his efforts met with little success. In 1722 he broke with her completely, possibly on account of her jealousy of Stella. It was popularly believed that her death the following year resulted from her shock at this breach. For Swift's early efforts to humor their relationship, see his poem "Cadenus and Vanessa," written probably in 1713 and privately kept in manuscript until copies were somehow circulated in 1723, in the wake of her death and amid scandalous rumors concerning her relationship with Swift.

11 the soul none dare forgive: Because of the rebarbative nature of his satire, Swift was reviled as no other major English author had been or has been since. That he felt these attacks is evident in the epitaph he wrote for himself, in which he says that in death he is *Ubi saeva indignatio ulterius cor lacerare nequit* ("Where savage indignation no more can lacerate his heart").

"In whose will is our peace?"

According to Cunningham's copy of *CPE*, begun in Santa Barbara in August 1941 and finished in Palo Alto in January of 1944. (Gullans lists just the first half of the data.)

1 In whose will is our peace: An echo of Dante (*Paradiso*, 3.85): *E 'n la sua volontade è nostra pace* ("And in his will is our peace"). **5 And if I rest not till I rest in thee:** An echo of Saint Augustine (*Confessions*, 1.1): *inquietum est cor nostrum, donec requiescat in te* ("restless is our heart, until it rests in thee"). In expressing both a hunger for religious faith and a difficulty in believing, this poem, which closes *JF*, resembles "The Phoenix," which opens the collection.

Doctor Drink (1950)

In the Thirtieth Year

Written in Chicago in 1947 or 1948. (In his copy of *CPE*, Cunningham's note reads specifically, "Winter '47?, '48? | Chicago.")

Interview with Doctor Drink

Written in Chicago; begun in September 1949, continued in December of that year, and evidently finished in January 1950. (In his copy of *CPE,* Cunningham puts a question mark before "Jan. '50.")

2 transference: In psychoanalysis, the patient's shifting of emotions from one person or object to another, especially the shifting of emotions about a parent to the therapist. Apparently the speaker of the poem is shifting his bitter feelings about love and life to the bottle of liquor—the fifth of therapy. Even if one doubts the efficacy of psychoanalysis, its therapy is probably more beneficial than the alternative depicted here.

"Lip was a man"

No place-and-date-of-composition listing in Gullans, and Cunningham's note for the poem, in his copy of *CPE,* simply reads "Chicago," where he lived in the late 1940s. The epigram was first published in *DD* (1950). Ben Jonson wrote an epigram entitled "On Lippe, the Teacher" (*Epigrams,* 75), and when Cunningham named his protagonist, he may have been alluding to or remembering Jonson's poem:

> I cannot think there's that antipathy
> 'Twixt Puritans and players, as some cry;
> Though Lippe, at Paul's, ran from his text away
> T'inveigh 'gainst plays, what did he then but play?

"Reader, it's time reality was faced"

No place-and-date-of-composition listing in Gullans. *DD* (1950) marks the epigram's first appearance—and last, in Cunningham's lifetime. He did not reprint this epigram in either *ER* or *CPE.*

2 My verse is naughty but my life is chaste: A proverbial disclaimer of and about authors of satirical poetry. See Martial, 1.4.8: *lasciva est nobis pagina, vita proba* ("Lascivious is my page, but my life is virtuous"); and Hadrian 2, "On Voconius": *Lascivus versu, mente pudicus eras* ("Lascivious was your verse, but your mind was modest").

Epitaph for Someone or Other

No place-and-date-of-composition listing in Gullans, and Cunningham, in his copy of *CPE,* simply notes of the poem, "Chicago." Since *DD* (1950) marks the poem's first appearance, and since Cunningham lived in Chicago in the late 1940s, the poem was likely written in 1948 or 1949. Gullans notes, in his working copy of *CPE,* that the epigram is a variation on one of Palladas's (*Palatine Anthology,* 10.58):

> Gês epebēn gumnos, gumnos th' hupo gaian apeimi;
> kai ti matēn mochthō, gumnon horōn to telos?

Naked I alighted on the earth and naked I shall go beneath it. Why do I toil in vain, seeing the end is nakedness? (trans. W. R. Paton)

"All in due time"

Written in Chicago in June 1949.

"Dear child whom I begot"

According to Gullans, written in Balboa in fall 1942 or spring 1943. Cunningham himself notes, in his copy of *CPE,* " '42?, '43? | Balboa."

"Life flows to death"

No place-and-date-of-composition listing in Gullans, and Cunningham, in his working copy of *CPE,* merely notes of the poem, "Chicago." Since *DD* (1950) marks the poem's first appearance, and since Cunningham lived in Chicago in the late 1940s, the poem was probably written, like the other undated poems in *DD,* in 1948 or 1949. This epigram translates one of John Owen's (1.32):

De Vita et Morte

> Ad mortem sic vita fluit, velut ad mare flumen:
> Vivere nam res est dulcis, amara mori.

Of Life and Death

To death thus life flows, even as does to the sea a river: for to live is a sweet thing, and to die is bitter.

"On a cold night"

Written in Chicago on February 14, 1950. In his working copy of *CPE,*

Gullans suggests that the opening line of the poem may echo the openings of two epigrams in the *Palatine Anthology* (5.120; 5.167). Both of these epigrams involve a lover who passes nocturnally through inclement weather, though they otherwise differ from Cunningham's epigram.

Trivial, Vulgar, and Exalted (1959)
Uncollected Poems and Epigrams

To avoid bibliographical confusion, one should mention that in 1957 Cunningham published a broadside (San Francisco: Poems in Folio) entitled *Trivial, Vulgar, and Exalted*. It contained "On *Doctor Drink*," "Night-piece," "New York: 5 March 1957," and "Good Fortune, When I Hailed Her." Two years later, when assembling *The Exclusions of a Rhyme,* he recycled the title of the broadside and grouped under it various poems and epigrams that he had written in the 1950s, as well as a few earlier pieces that he had not collected in *The Helmsman, The Judge Is Fury,* or *Doctor Drink.* Hence Cunningham's *oeuvre* has two groups of poems with the same title, the second encompassing and enlarging the first.

On Doctor Drink

Written in Sudbury, Massachusetts, in October 1956.

"Here lies my wife"

No place-and-date-of-composition listing in Gullans, and Cunningham, in his copy of *CPE,* places only a question mark under the poem. The epigram first appeared in Rolfe Humphries, ed., *New Poems by American Poets* (New York: Ballantine, 1953).

"My name is Ebenezer Brown"

No place-and-date-of-composition listing in Gullans, and Cunningham, in his copy of *CPE,* simply notes "Sudbury" under the poem. The epigram first appeared in *Partisan Review* 26 (Fall 1959). Since Cunningham moved to Sudbury in August of 1955, the epigram must have been written between that date and 1959. The epigram exemplifies another of the form's sub-genres, in this case the humorous epitaph that alludes to the subject's profession. X. J. Kennedy's "For a Postal Clerk" is another example of the type:

Here lies wrapped up tight in sod
Henry Harkins c/o God.
On the day of Resurrection
May be opened for inspection.

"I married in my youth"

Written in Sudbury in 1956.

"Here lies New Critic"

Written in Charlottesville, Virginia, in 1952 or 1953. This cleverly updates an epigram by John Hoskyns (1566–1638):

> *Hic jacet Egremundus Rarus,*
> *Tuendis paradoxis clarus.*
> *Mortuus est, ut hic apparet:*
> *At si loqui posset, hoc negaret.*

Here lies Egremundus Rarus, famous for his paradoxes. He is dead, as is plain: but if he could speak, he would surely deny it. (trans. Rebecka Lindau)

William Edinger (see Gullans, v) was the first to point out this source.

"You wonder why Drab"

No place-and-date-of-composition listing in Gullans, and Cunningham, in his copy of *CPE,* simply places a question mark beneath the poem. The epigram first appeared in Humphries, *New Poems by American Poets* (1953). Cunningham notes after his question mark, "Tr. Johannes Secundus," indicating that this epigram translates or adapts one from Johannes (also called Janus) Secundus (1511–1536):

> *Gellia miraris cur auro vendat amorem?*
> *Scilicet ut sit quo callida rursus emat.*

You wonder why Gellia sells for gold her love? Namely, so that the clever girl will be able someday to buy it back.

1 Drab: A prostitute. Of the word, the *OED* says: "Not known before 16th c.; derivation uncertain: prob. at first a low or cant word. Evidently connected with Irish *drabog,* Gael. *drabag* dirty female, slattern; but evidence is wanting to show which is the original."

"You ask me how Contempt"

Written in Seattle in summer 1956, according to Gullans. Cunningham, in his copy of *CPE,* simply notes, "'56? | Seattle?"

"With every wife he can, and you know why?"

Written in Seattle in summer 1956.

"Bride loved old words"

No place-and-date-of-composition listing in Gullans, and Cunningham, in his copy of *CPE,* simply places a question mark under the poem. The epigram first appeared in *Partisan Review* 26 (Fall 1959).

3 yard: See entry 11 for "**Yard** sb.²" in the *OED,* which reports the word is an obsolete form for "The virile member."

"Career was feminine"

No place-and-date-of-composition listing in Gullans, and Cunningham, in his copy of *CPE,* simply places a question mark under the poem. The epigram first appeared in *Partisan Review* 26 (Fall 1959).

"Your affair, my dear, need not be a mess"

No place-and-date-of-composition listing in Gullans, but Cunningham, in his copy of *CPE,* notes beneath the poem "Spring '59, | Sudbury." The epigram first appeared in *Partisan Review* 26 (Fall 1959).

5 Sir Gawain and the Fay: An allusion to the fourteenth-century narrative poem, *Sir Gawain and the Green Knight,* in which Gawain is tempted by the wizardess Morgan le Fay, posing as the wife of a lord who offers Gawain hospitality. Though Gawain and the Fay do not sleep together, they kiss on three successive days—once on the first day, twice on the second, three times on the third. On day three the Fay also gives Gawain her ceinture, telling him it will protect him from death. This gift is particularly welcome to Gawain because he is on his way to meet the Green Knight, to allow the latter to decapitate him, just as he had earlier decapitated the Green Knight, who, however, proved miraculously unharmed by the operation. Gawain's conduct with the Fay is thus, if not out-and-out dishonorable, a bit sneaky. (Gawain does inform the lord about kissing the lady, but says nothing of the ceinture. When Gawain eventually meets the Green Knight, the latter reveals that he, disguised, was the lord with whom Gawain was staying. The Green Knight spares Gawain's life on account of the honest element of his behavior, nicking his neck, however, with a battle-axe because Gawain did not tell him about the ceinture.)

"The Elders at their services"

No date-and-place-of-composition listing in Gullans, and Cunningham, in his copy of *CPE,* just sets a question mark under the epigram. The epigram first appeared in Humphries, *New Poems by American Poets* (1953). As he does in "The True Religion," Cunningham here treats psychoanalysis as a kind of latter-day Church with its own rites of initiation and articles of faith.

3 couches: A reference to the psychoanalyst's couch. In this case, the neophytes ("catechumens") are testifying and confessing not to their priest, but to their therapist.

"Arms and the man I sing"

No place-and-date-of-composition listing in Gullans, and Cunningham, in his copy of *CPE,* just sets a question mark under the epigram. The epigram first appeared in Humphries, *New Poems by American Poets* (1953).

1 Arms and the man I sing: A translation of the opening of *The Aeneid,* in which Virgil announces: *Arma virumque cano.*

"The man who goes for Christian resignation"

No place-and-date-of-composition listing in Gullans. The epigram first appeared in Humphries, *New Poems by American Poets* (1953). After collecting this epigram in *ER,* Cunningham did not include it in *CPE.*

"Another novel"

Written in Seattle in summer 1956.

"And now you're ready"

No place-and-date-of-composition listing in Gullans, and Cunningham, in his copy of *CPE,* just puts a question mark under the epigram. The epigram first appeared in 1960 in *ER*. It adapts and compresses a bawdy poem by Scythinus (*Palatine Anthology,* 12.232); in fact, Cunningham's epigram is reprinted as a translation in *The Greek Anthology and Other Ancient Epigrams: A Selection in Modern Verse Translation,* edited with an introduction by Peter Jay (London: Penguin, 1981).

For a College Yearbook

Written in Sudbury in May 1959.

"Love, receive Lais' glass"

No place-and-date-of-composition listing in Gullans, and Cunningham, in his copy of *CPE,* just sets a question mark under the epigram, which first appeared in 1960 in *ER*. The epigram adapts and compresses one of Plato's (*Palatine Anthology,* 6.1):

> *He sobaron gelasasa kath' Heladdos, hē pot' erastōn*
> *hesmon epi prothurois Lais echousa neōn,*
> *tei Paphiēi to katoptron; epei toiē men horasthai*
> *ouk ethelō, hoiē d' ēn paros ou dunamai.*

I, Lais, whose haughty beauty make mock of Greece, I who once had a swarm of young lovers at my doors, dedicate my mirror to Aphrodite, since I wish not to look on myself as I am, and cannot look on myself as I once was. (trans. W. R. Paton)

Matthew Prior's "The Lady Who Offers Her Looking-glass to Venus" is an earlier adaptation of the same epigram:

> Venus, take my votive glass:
> Since I am not what I was,
> What from this day I shall be,
> Venus, never let me see.

1 Lais: a Greek courtesan famous for her beauty. A number of epigrams about her appear in the *Palatine Anthology.*

"I had gone broke"

Written in Chicago on April 1, 1951.

4 By Hatred . . . Despair: The formulary way of describing the genealogy of a horse. In this case, the sire was Hatred and the mother was Envy and the grandsire was Despair.

"Friend, on this scaffold"

No place-and-date-of-composition listing in Gullans, and Cunningham, in his copy of *CPE,* puts a question mark under the epigram. The epigram first appeared in Humphries, *New Poems by American Poets* (1953). In front of his question mark, Cunningham notes "Tr. Owen, 2.152," indicating that he is adapting the 152nd epigram of the second book of John Owen's ten books of epigrams. It is interesting to see how Cunningham transforms and gives intellectual depth and seriousness to Owen's somewhat flat and anecdotal original:

Morus moriens

Abscindi passus caput est a corpore Morus;
Abscindi crines noluit a capite.

More dying

More suffered his head to be cut from his body; but did not wish his hair to be cut from his head.

1 Thomas More: More (1478-1535) was a gifted scholar and writer, who held important posts in Henry VIII's government. However, when More refused to endorse the king's efforts to repudiate the authority of the Pope and to establish control of the English Church, he was beheaded on a trumped-up charge of treason. Owen's epigram refers to a comment that More made just before he was decapitated. Laying his head on the block, he drew his beard aside and said to his executioner, "This hath not offended the king" (Francis Bacon, *Apothegms,* 22). **2 Who would not cut the body from the head:** More believed the Pope was the "Head" of the "Body" of the Church, and would not support Henry's attempt to sever the two. It is thus especially ironic that More, defending the spiritual and ecclesiatical unity of head and body, should himself suffer a physical and literal division of the same. More was canonized by the Catholic Church in 1935.

"And what is love?"

Written in Chicago on April 26, 1950.

Night-piece

Written in Concord, Massachusetts, in May 1955.

New York: 5 March 1957

According to Gullans, written in Sudbury in March 1957. In his copy of *CPE*, Cunningham lists only "Sudbury" beneath the poem.

"Good Fortune, when I hailed her"

Written in Sudbury in March 1956.

Fear

Written in Palo Alto in July of 1942. In his copy of *CPE*, Cunningham attaches a plus sign to the date, evidently to indicate that the poem was revised thereafter. When the poem first appeared, under the title of "To E. . . . ," in *New Mexico Quarterly Review* 13 (Autumn 1943), it had fifteen rather than nine lines:

> Love at what distance mine!
> On whose disdain I dine
> Unfed, unfamished, I
> In your hid counsels lie.
> I know your lover, fear.
> His presence is austere
> As winter air; he trembles
> At the interior thunder
> Of chill erotic wonder,
> Though the taut face dissembles:
> I know him, I am he.
>
> Stilled in his arms, my dear,
> In tenderness of fear,
> Fulfilled of terror, sleep!
> And though you cannot, weep!

For the final version of the poem, Cunningham excised lines eight and nine and the last four lines.

The Aged Lover Discourses in the Flat Style

Written in Sudbury, c. 1958, according to Gullans. In his copy of *CPE,* Cunningham lists only "Sudbury" beneath the poem.

Horoscope

Begun in 1945 in Honolulu (though Cunningham places a question mark after the city's name), continued in 1952 in Cambridge, Massachusetts, and completed in 1958 in Sudbury. The poem was essentially finished by 1952, and Cunningham published it that year in the October issue of *Poetry.* This version differs little from the final version, except that a first-person pronominal appears in places in the first half of the poem where Cunningham would later substitute an impersonal pronoun:

> Out of my birth
> The magi chart my worth;
> They mark the influence
> Of hour and day; they weigh what thence

> Must come to me.
> I in their cold sky see
> No Venus and no Mars . . .

7 Venus . . . Mars: The Roman deities of Love and War, respectively. The speaker of the poem sees in his future neither amorous nor martial exploits.

Prefatory Poem to The Exclusions of a Rhyme (1960)

To My Wife

Written in Sudbury in August 1958. Cunningham married Jessie MacGregor Campbell on June 3, 1950. They were husband and wife until his death in 1985.

To What Strangers, What Welcome (1964)

A Sequence of Short Poems

In his essay "Several Kinds of Short Poem," Cunningham writes of *To What Strangers, What Welcome:*

I had entertained the general notion of . . . a sequence [of short poems] for many years and had designated the areas of experience that would be involved. The poems would deal with the American West, that vast spiritual region from Great Falls, Montana, to El Paso, Texas; from Fort Riley, Kansas, to the sinks of Nevada; and with the California Coast, another and perhaps less spiritual region. And the poems would relate some sort of illicit and finally terminated love affair. And there would be a fusion of the feeling in the personal relationship and the feeling for the West and the Coast. (*CE*, 435)

Cunningham adds that he wished the sequence to be narrative rather than simply a group of related poems, such as Propertius's *Elegies* or the sonnet cycles of the Renaissance. Cunningham summarizes the plot of his sequence thus: "A traveler drives west; he falls in love; he comes home" (*CE*, 435). Because the sequence is elliptical, some readers may appreciate the following outline:

#1: protagonist drives west, has intimation of an as-yet-unmet lover

#2: description of a stop on the way

#3: a meditation on sexual passion, its nature and meaning

#4: "an unsent letter, meditated at midnight, to no one at all" (*CE*, 436)

#5: the first of two "unrewarding adventures" (*CE*, 437)—a pick-up at a bar

#6: the second of the unrewarding adventures—a show in Las Vegas

#7: protagonist arrives at the Pacific

#8: description of the protagonist living at house on beach

#9: protagonist falls in love; the affair begins

#10: protagonist and lover share an evening

#11: protagonist heads east; decision to end the affair has been made

#12: protagonist feels the absence of the beloved as he crosses the desert and the Midwest ("prairie") and returns to New England ("stonewalled road")

#13: comment on the reality and finality of acts and words

#14: the love affair remembered

#15: a meditation on the tenuousness of our lives and on the providential dispensation that life goes on, regardless of our personal interests in arresting its processes or in clinging to the past

Epigraph

The epigraph from Robinson's *Merlin* occurs at that point in the poem when Merlin has left his beloved Vivian and returned to Arthur's disintegrating court in an ultimately futile attempt to save it. Merlin foresees that he himself is doomed and will never look on Vivian again. Cunningham did not include the epigraph when he reprinted *TWSWW* in *CPE*. I have restored the epigraph because it is memorable and anticipates the nature and feeling of Cunningham's sequence.

1 "I drive Westward"

Begun in Sheridan, Wyoming, in August 1959 and completed in Chicago in October 1959.

2 "On either side of the white line"

Written in Tucson, Arizona, on January 5, 1960.

3 "In a few days now"

Begun at Yaddo, New York, on May 5, 1960 and completed in Santa Barbara on April 16, 1963.

4 "You have here no otherness"

Written in a train from New York City to the Route 128 stop outside Boston on March 19, 1962. This is the first of the poems in the sequence—the others are #7, #9, #10, and #14—in purely syllabic meter. In this case, each line has seven syllables but no recurrent pattern of feet or accents.

5 "The soft lights, the companionship, the beers"

Written in Palo Alto in February 1960. When first published in *Partisan Review* 27 (Fall 1960) and when collected in *TWSWW* (1964), this poem carried the title "The Pick-up."

6 "It was in Vegas"

Written in Santa Fe, New Mexico, in March 1960.

7 "A traveller, the highway my guide"

Written in Santa Fe on March 18, 1960. The meter is syllabic, nine syllables per line, with no recurring pattern of feet or accents. The meter directs that we should read "moseying" as disyllabic, with the second syllable of the word syncopated: mos'ying. In his essay "How Shall the Poem Be Written," Cunningham indicates that he regards the conventional forms of elision as being a part of syllabic verse: "In the modern tradition it [syllabic verse] has these rules: the syllabification is that of ordinary educated speech, not of careful enunciation, and elision is optional" (CE, 260).

#8 "The night is still"

Begun on April 29, 1963, and completed May 1, 1963, in Santa Barbara. The poem's meter might be called mini-Miltonic—unrhymed iambic tetrameter. Initial confusion may result if we do not perceive that the third foot of the first line involves an elision:

x /   x /   > / x /

The night | is still. | The *un*fail | ing surf

#9 "Innocent to innocent"

Begun on May 29, 1963, and completed on June 4, 1963, in Santa Barbara. The poem's meter is syllabic—seven syllables per line, with no recurring pattern of feet or accents.

#10 "A half hour for coffee"

According to Cunningham's copy of CPE, begun on July 2, 1963, in Santa Fe and completed on July 4, 1963, in Roy, New Mexico. Gullans's listings for this poem ("July 2, 1963, Santa Fe, Roy, New Mexico") and for the following one ("July 4, 1963, Santa Fe, Roy, New Mexico") seem to reflect a miscommunication between him and Cunningham. Roy is approximately a hundred miles northeast of Santa Fe, and it is unlikely that Cunningham was commuting between the two towns. Rather, as his own notes suggest, he was probably in Santa Fe on July 2 and by July 4 had traveled up to Roy. This poem's meter is syllabic—nine syllables per line, but with no recurrent pattern of feet or accents.

#11 "I drive Eastward"

According to Cunningham's copy of CPE, written on July 4, 1963 in Roy. About the evidently confused listing in Gullans, see note immediately above.

2 coyotes: The meter indicates that the word is to be read as a fore-stressed disyllable ("kí yotes") rather than as a middle-stressed trisyllable ("ki yó tes").

#12 *"Absence, my angel"*

Written in Sudbury on July 21, 1963.

#13 "Nescit vox missa reverti . . ."

Written in Sudbury on July 16, 1963. The title comes from Horace's caution against publishing too hastily: "The word sent forth can never return" *(Ars Poetica,* 390).

#14 *"I write only to say this"*

Written in Sudbury on October 1, 1963. The meter is syllabic, as Cunningham indicates in the poem's second line. Each line line has seven syllables, with no recurring pattern of feet or accents.

#15 *"Identity, that spectator"*

Written in Sudbury on October 14, 1963. The meter is unrhymed iambic tetrameter.

Poems and Epigrams (1960–1970)

Cunningham first collected most of the work in this section in *Some Salt* (Madison, Wisc.: Perishable Press, 1967); however, four of the epigrams and "Montana Fifty Years Ago" did not appear in a book until *CPE.* The sequence of materials here follows the arrangement Cunningham adopted for *SS.* The additional epigrams have been inserted between "An Oedipean Mom and Dad" and "I, Too, Have Been to the Huntington"; and "Montana Fifty Years Ago" has been tacked on at the end.

"I write you in my need"

Written in San Gabriel, California, and Santa Fe in 1960.

"Illusion and delusion"

Written in Sudbury on August 26 (?)—the question mark is Cunningham's—in 1966.

For a Woman with Child

Written in Sudbury in 1965, according to Cunningham's copy of *CPE*. Gullans gives the date as 1966.

"Old love is old resentment"

Written in Santa Barbara in winter 1967.

Towards Tucson

Written in Tucson on December 9, 1966.

"There is a ghost town"

Written in Sudbury on May 1966.

On a Line from Bodenham's "Belvedere"

Written in Sudbury on August 23, 1962. Little is known of John Bodenham (fl. 1600), but his name is associated with several early miscellanies of English verse. The best known of these is *England's Helicon* (1600). Others include the work to which Cunningham refers, *Belvedére, or the Garden of the Muses* (1600), a kind of dictionary of short verse quotations. Some scholars believe that Bodenham actually compiled these miscellanies; others believe that he simply projected them or underwrote their production. The line that Cunningham cites may be found in *Bodenham's Belvedére,* reprint of 1600 edition (New York: Burt Franklin, 1967), 55.

"Who am I?"

Written in Sudbury on December 7, 1962.

"I grow old"

No place-and-date-of-composition listing in Gullans, and Cunningham, in his copy of *CPE,* merely writes a question mark under the epigram. It initially appeared in *The Southern Review* 3 (Autumn 1967) and in *SS* (also Autumn 1967).

"Young Sensitive one summer on the Cape "

Written in Sudbury on August 24, 1962.

1 the Cape: Readers from outside the United States may appreciate being told that this refers to Cape Cod, a popular resort region on the Massachusetts coast. During summer break from school, many college students from the Boston area work on the Cape at restaurants, shops, and other tourist-related establishments.

Love's Progress

Written in Sudbury on May 10, 1961.

"Mistress of scenes, good-by"

Written in Sudbury on May 13, 1961.

Modern Love

Finished in Sudbury in June 1967, though the note in Cunningham's copy of *CPE*—"?–June '67"—indicates that the poem was begun some time earlier. The title may ironically allude to George Meredith's *Modern Love* (1862), a somber sequence of poems that records the misunderstandings and sexual misadventures of a collapsing marriage.

"Prue loved her man"

Like "Illusion and delusion," written in Sudbury on August 26 (?)—the question mark is Cunningham's—in 1966.

"A faint smile of distraction"

Written in Sudbury in summer 1966.

"An Oedipean Mom and Dad"

No place-and-date-of-composition listing in Gullans, and Cunningham, in his copy of *CPE,* merely puts a question mark under the epigram. It first appeared in *SS* (1967).

"Some twenty years of marital agreement"

Written in Sudbury in 1967.

"A periphrastic insult"

Written in Sudbury in August 1962.

Portrait

Written in Sudbury on August 4, 1963.

On a Letter

Written in Sudbury on August 14, 1965.

I, Too, Have Been to the Huntington

Cunningham's note about the place and date of composition reads "Feb. 7, '60 | North on 101 to Pismo Beach." (Pismo Beach is on the California coast and is approximately a hundred miles north of Santa Barbara.) "The Huntington" is the Huntington Library in San Marino, California. The institution has, in addition to its collection of rare books and manuscripts, beautiful gardens and art galleries.

   1 railroad baron: Henry E. Huntington (1850–1927) was a major book collector and established and endowed the Huntington Library. He was the nephew of Collis Potter Huntington (1821–1900), the notorious railroad developer and "robber baron." Cunningham may have confused the two men, but he may also be referring, in the lines "With someone else's pick and shovel / Built this hovel," to the fact that Henry worked for his uncle for many years and on the latter's death inherited much of his wealth, wealth later used to buy books and art and to create the Huntington.

The True Religion

Written in Sudbury in fall (?)—the question mark is Cunningham's—of 1961. Like "I showed some Devils of a moral kind," "The Elders at their services begin," "Interview with Doctor Drink," and "An Oedipean Mom and Dad," this poem comments satirically on Freud or Freudianism. The poem may have been stimulated in part by John Osborne's *Luther*, which was produced in the same year Cunningham wrote the poem and which offered a Freudian interpretation of Martin Luther.

   1 Religion: Many have debated whether Freud's theories represent a science or a mythology. Here Cunningham suggests that the values of psycho-analysis (or a popularized, banalized version of it) are replacing those of Judeo-Christian ethics. **3–4 Freudly Reformation . . . translation:** Freud is compared to Luther (1483–1546), who broke with the Church of Rome and founded Protestantism. A key element in Luther's Reformation was his translation of the Old and New Testaments into German. Essential to the Reformed Church was its community of independent believers committed to examining religious matters for themselves. Such a community could not exist until the Bible was made accessible to people who knew only a vernacular language. The translation of Freud to which Cunningham refers may be James Strachey's *Standard Edition of Freud's Works* (24 vols., 1953–1973). Or the reference may be to *The Interpretation of Dreams,* which was originally published in German in 1899 and first appeared in English in A. A. Brill's translation of 1913. **5–10 Their fear . . . panic:** A list of virtues reinterpreted in light of psychoanalytic theory. What was fear of God for our ancestors has become "anxiety" for us. Things that were "virtuous" for them, we now regard as manifestations of self-repression. And so on. **15 He does . . . is heard:** The patient is ignorant of the sources of his behavior; he is "heard" by his psychotherapist. **16 transferred and untransferred:** see the note to "Interview with Doctor Drink" on "transference."

Monday Morning

Written in Sudbury on January 11, 1965. The poem's meter is syllabic—nine syllables per line, with no regular pattern of feet or accents.

Consolatio Nova

Written in Sudbury on May 13 and 14, 1967. The title is Latin for "Modern Consolation." The consolation offered by the poem is modern since it does not entail the conventional Christian faith that, though we die, our flesh will ultimately be resurrected so that we may join each other and Christ in Heaven. Alan Swallow (1915–1966) founded the Swallow Press in 1940 and was Cunningham's principal publisher from *JF* onward.

6 monads: According to Pythagorean doctrine, the monad is the most fundamental unit of the universe. Diogenes Laertius summarizes (8.25 [Pythagoras]) the doctrine:

> The principle of all things is the monad or unit (*monada*); arising from this monad the undefined dyad or two serves as material substratum to the monad,

which is cause; from the monad and the undefined dyad spring numbers; from numbers, points; from points, lines; from lines, plane figures; from plane figures, solid figures; from solid figures, sensible bodies, the elements of which are four, fire, water, earth and air; these elements interchange and turn into one another completely, and combine to produce a universe animate, intelligent, spherical. (Diogenes Laertius, *Lives of Eminent Philosophers,* 2 vols., trans. R. D. Hicks [LCL] Cambridge, Mass.: Harvard University Press, 1972)

Gottfried Wilhelm von Leibniz (1646-1716) is the modern philosopher most closely associated with the concept of the monad. In his late *Monadology* (1714), he argued that monads were simple, soul-like substances that join compositely with other monads to form things and that humans were essentially collections of monads. **8 A causeless . . . somes:** Leibniz believed that monads—and by extension life—were, after being initially created, determined by the laws of cause and effect. Cunningham seems to suggest in this line that people, though their individual existences are momentary and subject to causality, are ultimately one with God or with that Principle of Being that causes things, but that is Itself beyond causality (the "causeless all").

Think

Begun in Sudbury in January 1965 and completed in Sudbury on May 30, 1967. The poem's meter is syllabic—seven syllables per line, with no pattern of feet or accents.

Montana Fifty Years Ago

Begun in Sudbury in summer 1966 and completed in Sudbury on October 12, 1967. Cunningham once said that this poem refers to the dry-land ranch where he went each summer while growing up in Montana. "[T]he poem 'Montana Fifty Years Ago' is an attempt to summarize not so much my own experience, but to put into form the kind of situation out at the ranch" (Steele, "Interview with J.V. Cunningham," 4).

Late Epigrams (1970–1982)

Cunningham collected for *Let Thy Words Be Few* the epigrams in this section, and had he not died before the book's appearance, he might well have listed in a copy of it when and where the contents had been composed. As it is, we for the most part can only guess at this information. However, the final six epigrams in this section were published in John Hazel Smith, ed., *Brandeis Essays in Literature* (Waltham: Brandeis University, 1983), and when they appeared, a date of composition was printed beneath each. (Two of these epigrams also appeared, with dates of composition, as a broadside in Kathy Walkup's Chimera Broadsides, Series II, 1983.) Of the remaining epigrams in this section, a number initially appeared in *The New Republic* 182 (February 9, 1980). One appeared in *Counter/Measures* in 1972 and another in *Ploughshares* in 1975. Two others were not published until *LTWBF* in 1988. In view of Cunningham's working habits and publishing history, it is probable all of the epigrams, with the exception of "They" (see the note below for this poem) were written after 1970. It is also conceivable, however, that he had had some of the work on hand for some time and never took the occasion to put it in finished form or to publish it until this fairly late period of his career.

Regarding the epigrams first published in *The New Republic*, a future editor or bibliographer of Cunningham might appreciate knowing that the texts are not, as they appear in that magazine, altogether reliable. Someone at *The New Republic* made several last-minute alterations in the epigrams without consulting Cunningham. As Cunningham explained when he submitted the manuscript of *LTWBF* to Gullans, its texts of *The New Republic* poems "restore the original readings, as I saw them in proof. The changes [that appeared in *The New Republic*] are improvements at the last moment by an editor at *NR*, who in fact called me just before press time in Santa Barbara to query other details, but silent on these. I offer the poems to you unimproved" (J.V. Cunningham, letter to Charles Gullans, undated but postmarked 1 March 1985).

"Some good, some middling, and some bad"

No place-and-date-of-composition listing in Gullans. The epigram was first published in *The New Republic* 182 (February 9, 1980). As the subscripted indicates, the epigram is based on Martial's two-liner:

> *Sunt bona, sunt quaedam mediocria, sunt mala plura*
> *quae legis hic. aliter no fit, Avite, liber.*

There are good poems, there are a number of so-so ones, there are a greater number of bad that you read here. Not otherwise is it possible to make, Avitus, a book.

"Who lives by wisdom"

No place-and-date-of-composition in Gullans. The epigram was first published in *The New Republic* 182 (February 9, 1980).

The Lights of Love

No place-and-date-of-composition listing place in Gullans. The epigram was first published in *The New Republic* 182 (February 9, 1980).

On Correggio's Leda

No place-and-date-of-composition listing in Gullans. The epigram first appeared in *The New Republic* 182 (February 9, 1980). Called "Correggio" after his native town in Northern Italy, Antonio Allegri (1494–1534) is one of the master-painters of the High Renaissance.

Gnothi Seauton

No place-and-date-of-composition listing in Gullans. The epigram first appeared in *The New Republic* 182 (February 9, 1980). The title is the Greek proverb "Know thyself." Plato reports (*Protagoras* 343B) it was inscribed on the temple at Delphi, and Juvenal quotes it in *Satires*, 11.27: *E cielo descendit Gnōthi seauton* ("From heaven descended the advice *Know thyself*").

Memoir

No place-and-date-of-composition listing in Gullans. The epigram was first published in *The New Republic* 182 (February 9, 1980).

Original Sin

No place-and-date-of-composition listing in Gullans. The epigram was first published in *The New Republic* 182 (February 9, 1980).

"I have come home"

No place-and-date-of-composition listing in Gullans. The epigram was first published in *The New Republic* 182 (February 9, 1980). As the subscripted note indicates, the epigram adapts the following anonymous piece in the *Palatine Anthology:*

> *Elpis kai su, Tuche, mega chairete; ton limen' heuron;*
> *ouden emoi ch' humin; paixete tous met' eme.*

Farewell, Hope and Fortune, a long farewell. I have found the haven. I have no more to do with you. Make game of those who come after me. (trans. W. R. Paton)

They

No place-and-date-of-composition listing in Gullans, though Cunningham, on the recto of the last blank leaf of his copy of *CPE,* notes: " 'They', 1965." Evidently, he wrote the poem at that time and may at some point have considered including it in *CPE.* The epigram initially appeared in *Counter/Measures* 1 (1972).

2 Remains one deity: When all the other gods have been banished, the one that is left is, of course, The Self.

Cantor's Theorem: In an Infinite Class the Whole Is No Greater Than Some of Its Parts

No place-and-date-of-composition listing in Gullans. The epigram initially appeared, with the title "The Old Mathematics and the New," in *Ploughshares* 2, no. 4 (1975).

1 Euclid: Euclid (fl. c. 300 B.C.) lived and taught in Alexandria, where he composed his thirteen books of *Elements,* which deal with geometry and the theory of numbers. **3 Cantor:** Georg Cantor (1845–1918) is the great Russo-German mathematician who discovered or pointed out paradoxes in the concept and mathematics of the infinite. The one to which Cunningham evidently refers is that infinite sets may simultaneously correspond and differ. Imagine, for example, that line X_1 moves in one direction from point A to infinity, then imagine that line X_2 moves from point A in the opposite direction to infinity, and then imagine that line X_3 comprehends them both—moving, that is, through point A in both directions to infinity:

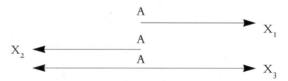

Line X_3 is the sum of lines X_1 and X_2. However, lines X_1 and X_2 are both infinite, greater than which nothing can be. Hence each equals X_3, which is also infinite. The whole is the sum of the two parts; and yet each part is also, as Cunningham puts it, equal to the whole. (Cantor's life and thought are discussed by Joseph Warren Dauben, *Georg Cantor: His Mathematics and Philosophy of the Infinite* [Princeton: Princeton University Press, 1979].)

"*If one takes trouble to explain*"

No place-and-date-of-composition listing in Gullans. The epigram first appeared in *LTWBF* (1988).

5 reasoning. The text of *LTWBF* has a comma rather than a period at the end of the line; however, Cunningham's manuscript has a period—a thick period, but a period—clearly distinguishable from his long and pronounced commas. (Because Cunningham died a month after sending off the manuscript of *LTWBF*, he never had the chance to read galleys for the collection.)

"*They said the Muses were but Nine*"

No place-and-date-of-composition listing in Gullans. The epigram first appeared in *LTWBF* (1988). As its subscripted note indicates, the epigram adapts the following poem, attributed to Plato, in the *Palatine Anthology:*

> *Ennea tas Mousas phasin tines: hōs oligōrōs;*
> *enude kai Sappho Lesbothen hē dekatē*

> Some say the Muses are nine, but how carelessly! Look at the tenth, Sappho from Lesbos. (trans. W. R. Paton)

Plato's epigram consists of a single elegiac couplet—a dactylic hexameter followed by a dactylic pentameter. To suggest the second-line-a-foot-shorter-than-the-first meter of the original, Cunningham has translated the epigram into an English iambic pentameter followed by an iambic tetrameter.

1 Muses: The nine daughters of Mnemosyne, goddess of memory, and Zeus. The Muses were thought by the Greeks to preside over the musico-poetical arts. **2 Sappho:** The popular lyric poet of ancient Greece. For additional information on Sappho (c. 612–c. 565 B.C.), see the note for her in the Translations section below.

A Few Words, and Some His,
In Memory of Clayton Stafford

Written, evidently in Sudbury, in June 1981. Clayton Stafford was a businessman and poet who was part of a circle of writers associated in the 1930s with Yvor Winters. Stafford published two books, *Verse 1931–1938* (Albuquerque: Swallow, 1941) and *The Swan and the Eagle and Other Poems* (San Francisco: Wesley Tanner, 1974). The second book includes and slightly enlarges the contents of the first. The poem of Stafford's to which Cunningham alludes is "Petrarchan Sonnet: Laura in Life":

> I had not known the silence of all speech,
> Word's waste of sense, talk's poverty, that hand
> Or eye or curving lip must dare command
> Meaning that strains beyond all verbal reach.
> I had not known that soon all words impeach
> Love's essence, muteness, (intricate demand!)
> Nor how, like shadow by the noon-day banned,
> Infusible our selves keep each from each.
>
> These things, I say, I had not known until—
> My own immeshed beneath their gazing weight—
> Your eyes stood full upon me, tender, still,
> Then left me sullen in my gross estate,
> As gulled by words my voice rushed forth to chill
> Love's naked presence, speech immaculate.

1 Corinthians 13: Commentary

Written, evidently in Sudbury, on August 1, 1982. This epigram alludes to Paul's discussion of love and to his remarks in verses 7 and 13 of 1 Corinthians 13: "Love bears all things, believes all things, hopes all things, endures all things. . . . So faith, hope, love abide, these three; but the greatest of these is love."

Statistics

Written, evidently in Sudbury, in 1980. The epigram makes, in a lighter hearted vein, the point made in "Meditation on Statistical Method."

Jack and Jill

Written, evidently in Sudbury, on February 3, 1981.

Somnium Narrare, Vigilantis Est

Written, evidently in Sudbury, on September 13, 1982. The sentence Cunningham takes from Seneca's fifty-third Epistle appears in Seneca's discussion of the necessity of our waking to a sense of our moral failings so as to correct them by means of philosophy:

> [T]he worse a person is, the less he feels it. You needn't feel surprised, my dearest Lucilius; a person sleeping lightly perceives impressions in his dreams and is sometimes, even, aware during sleep that he is asleep, whereas a heavy slumber blots out even dreams and plunges the mind too deep for consciousness of self. Why does no one admit his failings? Because he's still deep in them. It's the person who's awakened who recounts his dream, and acknowledging one's failings is a sign of health. (Seneca, *Letters from a Stoic,* selected and trans. with an introduction by Robin Campbell [New York: Penguin, 1969], 102)

To Whom It May Concern

Written, evidently in Sudbury, on December 1, 1980.

TRANSLATIONS (1932–1981)

SAPPHO

Sappho (c. 612–c. 565 B.C.) published nine books of odes, elegies, and epithalamia. One of her poems—the Aphrodite Ode—survives in its entirety, thanks to its having been quoted by Dionysius of Halicarnassus (*On Literary Composition,* 23). Another poem has come down to us in near complete form, thanks to its having been quoted by Longinus (*On the Sublime,* 10.2). Cunningham translates both of these. Various other fragments exist. The standard edition of Sappho is E. Lobel and Denys Page, eds., *Poetarum Lesbiorum Fragmenta* (Oxford: Oxford University Press, 1955). When Cunningham gives, above a poem or fragment of Sappho's, a note like "LP, Fr. 147," he is indicating that the item is the 147th fragment in Lobel and Page's edition. Cunningham first published "LP, 1" in *Canto* 3 (January 1981); "LP, Fr. 31" first appeared as a broadside from the Pomegranate

Press in Cambridge, Massachusetts, in 1973; "LP, Fr. 130" and "LP, Fr. 147" first appeared in *LTWBF.* Presently, most scholars reject the attribution to Sappho of *"Deduke men a selanna,"* though it is one of the best known fragments associated with her. Cunningham's translation of the fragment first appeared, along with a little essay entitled "A Few Remarks on Translating," in *Inscape* 36 (1981). Approximating the original Sapphic strophe—which involves four lines, the first three having eleven syllables and the fourth having five—Cunningham translates LP1 and LP, Fr. 31 in four-line stanzas whose syllable-count sequence runs 9, 9, 9, 5. Occasionally, the syllable count is maintained by an elision, as in

1 >3 4 5 6 7 8 9
With deity, the man who sits over

Cunningham renders *"Deduke men a selanna"* in iambic trimeter: "the lines are each of six syllables, and unobtrusively iambic" ("A Few Remarks on Translating," *Inscape,* 41). Where, in these notes, no comment is made about the meter of a translation, the reader may assume that Cunningham is working fairly obviously in one of the conventional English measures. For a discussion of Cunningham's versification generally, see Appendix B.

DECIMUS LABERIUS

Decimus Laberius (c. 115–43 B.C.) was a popular writer of mimes, of which only fragments survive. *The Oxford Classical Dictionary* reports: "Women acted in his plays for the first time in Rome." According to Macrobius (*Saturnalia,* 2.7), Laberius's outspoken political criticism angered Caesar, who in 45 B.C. forced the aging playwright to act in his own mimes. In "An Old Actor," which was spoken by Laberius from the stage before an audience that included Caesar, the poet wryly and ambiguously repents his attacks on the dictator. In writing his address, Laberius used the senarius—a line of six iambs. In imitation of this meter Cunningham casts his translation in iambic hexameters, taking here and there small liberties with the measure. Gullans dates the translation "ca. 1935." Cunningham initially published "An Old Actor" in *New Mexico Quarterly Review* 16 (Summer 1946). The translation was reprinted in L. R. Lind, ed., *Latin Poetry in Verse Translation* (Boston: Houghton Mifflin, 1958) and appeared later in *ER* and *CPE.*

CATULLUS

Gaius Valerius Catullus (c. 84–c. 54 B.C.) wrote in a wide range of the short forms—elegy, epistle, hymn, and epigram—and he inspired and influenced subsequent writers, from Virgil and Horace to the great vernacular poets of the Renaissance and beyond. Many of his poems, including the one Cunningham here translates, concern his unhappy love affair with Lesbia. (In real life, she was a woman named Clodia, a member of one the most politically and socially powerful families in Rome.) The number over Cunningham's translation indicates that the poem is the eighty-fifth in standard editions of Catullus. Cunningham first published this translation in *CPE* (1971).

HORACE

Quintus Horatius Flaccus (65–8 B.C.) is best known for his four books of *Odes* and his *Art of Poetry*. The number over Cunningham's translation indicates that the poem is the ninth of the first book in standard editions of Horace's *Odes*. Gullans dates the translation "1933," though Cunningham did not publish it until 1950, when Swallow issued "The Quest of the Opal" as a chapbook, with additional mimeographed pages containing the poems discussed in the essay. Cunningham reports that he modeled "The Helmsman: An Ode" on Horace's poem. Cunningham says of Horace in general and Horace's ode in particular:

> [The] Helmsman was . . . an imitation of Horace in its method. The qualities he then saw in the Horatian ode were conceived of in contrast with the medieval Latin lyric, with which he identified, not wholly correctly, his native style. The latter he found uncompromisingly rational and logical in structure and detail. In the former he discerned a unity of sensibility which exhibited the vagaries and unpredictability of experience and resisted an abstract, logical, or classificatory form. Its unity resided in the unformulable feeling that, as the poem unfolded, its length and arrangement of parts were proper and inevitable: "that just now is said what just now ought to be said." He found that the progression from detail to detail was by a kind of imagic shift or transformation image which, like a train through a tunnel, brings one to a new prospect on the other side of the divide. . . . But as he read on in Horace he came to see that the point of the method lay in the transitions from concrete detail to detail: that the transitions were not elliptical in the sense that the poet had merely omitted a chain of thought which the reader was to supply, and that the details themselves did not imply an abstraction that connected them. The meaning lay in the transitions themselves, in a certain balance of sensibility, a nice adjustment between imagery

and statement which met the insoluble problems of life with a controlled use of distraction and irrelevance.

He analyzed the famous Soracte ode (1.9) which begins with an extended description of a midwinter scene and closes with an extended, but in no way parallel, description of a summer love scene. By a relative clause, and in an un-emphatic manner, a description of the equinoctial storms is worked in. The sequence of images gives by implication, but by implication only, the theme: that season follows season, and that time is fleeting. The transitions from image to image are effected by generalized statements that are related to but never state the central theme, so that the point of the poem is qualified by images, whole and concrete in themselves, which cannot be said to illustrate the point. They are not subsumed under it as examples; they are rather digressions that prove to be developments.

He attempted to order the experience of his tradition by this method, and wrote his own ode ["The Helmsman"]. (*CE,* 419–20)

For his ode, Horace uses the Alcaic strophe, which involves four lines whose syl-lable-count sequence runs 11, 11, 9, 10. The stanza of Cunningham's translation involves two lines of eight syllables followed by one of seven and one of nine (though line four of the third stanza has only eight syllables). The lines of the translation can generally be scanned as conventionally iambic; however, the stanza's third line regularly has a feminine ending, and the third foot of the fourth line is regularly an anapest.

MARTIAL

Marcus Valerius Martialis (c. A.D. 40–c.104) is the best known writer of epi-grams in European literature. He published twelve books of epigrams and three additional books of epigrammatic-like verse—"On the Spectacles," and two collections of mottoes for "Guest-Gifts." The numbers over Cunningham's translations of Martial refer to standard editions of the poet and indicate the number of the book and epigram. Cunningham translated five of the Martial epigrams here—1.33, 2.5, 2.68, 4.69, and 6.65—in the course of translating Pierre Nicole, *An Essay on True and Apparent Beauty in Which from Settled Princi-ples is Rendered the Grounds for Choosing and Rejecting Epigrams* (Los Angeles: Au-gustan Reprint Society [William Andrew Clark Library], 1950). It was in *Latin Lines* (Detroit: Walter Hamady, 1965) that 2.4 first appeared, and it was in *CPE* (1971) that 1.32, 2.55, and 4.33 first appeared.

STATIUS

Publius Papinius Statius (c. A.D. 45–c. 96) is author of five books of *Silvae* or "Occasional Poems." (The title—the Latin word for "woods"—suggests a rough and miscellaneous forest-like abundance.) The number over Cunningham's translation refers to standard editions of the poet and indicates the number of the book and poem. This poem on sleep is Statius's most famous; Cunningham's translation of it first appeared in *YSW* 5 (May 1934), though the date of composition listed in Gullans is "1935."

HADRIAN

Publius Aelius Hadrianus (76–138) was Roman Emperor from 117 to his death. He both patronized and cultivated the arts and is said to have composed "Animula, vagula, blandula" (lit., "Little soul, little wanderer, little charmer") on his death bed just before he expired. Scholars have doubted this account, but it is a good story. Cunningham first published this translation in *LL* (1965).

SAINT AMBROSE

Ambrosius (c. 339–397) studied rhetoric, poetry, and law as a young man and, as Bishop of Milan, wrote a number of enduringly popular hymns. Indeed, Ambrose was to a considerable extent responsible for making music and song integral to the services in the Western Church. His hymns also played a key role in converting Augustine (*Confessions*, 9.6). Gullans dates this translation "1933 or 1934." The earlier date is probably more accurate, since the translation appeared in *YSW* 4 (June 1933). However, Cunningham subsequently made a number of slight revisions, and the second date may reflect the time of their incorporation.

THE ARCHPOET

Little is known of the Archpoet, whose title is a verbal analogue to the ecclesiastic title of his patron, Renaild of Dassel, the Archbishop of Cologne. The Archpoet lived in the twelfth century and is today the most celebrated of the goliards, the medieval wandering scholar-poets whose work is preserved chiefly in the *Carmina Burana*. Ten undisputed poems of the Archpoet survive, the most famous being the *Confessio*. (The title is not the poet's, but was attached to the poem in the thirteenth century.) The *Confessio* is addressed to the poet's patron,

and the reference, in the poem's title, to the poet's being "Bishop Golias" is iron-
ical. Golias is an eponym for "Goliard" and is the Latin form of Goliath's name.
"Golias" and "Goliard" may also be related to the Old·French *goliart,* meaning
"drunkard, glutton." Hence the Archpoet is a bishop of irreverence, barbarism,
and gluttony. Helen Waddell calls the poem "one of the hardest things in me-
dieval literature, the first articulate reasoned rebellion against the denying of the
body" *(Medieval Latin Lyrics,* reprint of 4th ed. of 1933 [London: Penguin, 1952],
339). Given Cunningham's experience as a wandering scholar, and his own
satirical outlook, this poem was a natural for him to translate. It is hard in Eng-
lish to approximate the Archpoet's stanza—a quatrain of thirteen-syllable lines
rhyming *aaaa.* In his translation, Cunningham employs a quatrain of four-beat
lines that freely mix disyllabic and trisyllabic feet, and he uses cross rhyme rather
than monorhyme. The translation, which omits several stanzas of the original, is
the earliest he preserved. Written in 1932 or 1933, it first appeared in *YSW* 4
(June 1933).

PIETRO BEMBO

Pietro Bembo (1470–1547) was a multitalented humanist from Venice who in
1539 was made a cardinal by Pope Paul III. Bembo's epitaph for Raphael can be
seen even today in the Pantheon in Rome, where the painter's remains rest in
an ancient Greek sarcophagus. Another fine if less exact translation of Bembo's
epitaph is Thomas Hardy's:

> Here's one in whom Nature feared—faint at such vying—
> Eclipse while he lived, and decease at his dying.
> ("Cardinal Bembo's Epitaph on Raphael")

Bembo's original runs:

> *Ille hic est Raphael, timuit quo sospite vinci*
> *Rerum magna parens, et moriente mori.*

This is that Raphael, whom our great parent, preserver of all things, feared to be
conquered by and feared to die with his dying.

Cunningham first published his translation in *LL* (1965).

JANUS VITALIS PANORMITANUS

Lind reports of this poet, "His Italian name was Giano Vitale (or Giovanni Vitali) and he was called Panormitanus because he was born at Palermo. His life falls in the last half of the fifteenth century; he is known chiefly for his short poems, many dedicated to contemporary writers" *(Latin Poetry in Verse Translation,* 384). Cunningham rendered Panormitanus's poem into English in the course of translating Nicole's *Essay on True and Apparent Beauty* (1950).

THOMAS MORE

Best known for his Latin-prose *Utopia,* Thomas More (1478–1535) was also a distinguished poet in both Latin and English. For additional comment on More, see the note above to "Friend, on this scaffold." Cunningham first published this translation of More in *CPE* (1971).

GEORGE BUCHANAN

George Buchanan (1506–1582) was a Scottish humanist, writer, traveler, and teacher. He had a colorful life. This included a professorship at Bordeaux, where Montaigne was one of his pupils, and two stints in prison in connection with religious controversies. Cunningham's three translations from Buchanan first appeared in *CPE* (1971).

Appendix A

Three Previously Uncollected Early Poems

In his twenties, especially, Cunningham published in periodicals a good deal of verse that he never gathered into his books. He was a sound if severe judge of his own work, and reading the uncollected poems, one understands why he decided not to reprint them. However, a number of these fugitive works are compelling, and readers may appreciate seeing a sample of them. Hence the three poems that follow—a Depression-era sonnet, a tribute to Wallace Stevens's *Harmonium,* and an experiment in epistolary verse. The last two of these poems suggest Cunningham's deep feeling for the Catholic tradition even as he was distancing himself from it. Stanzas six through nine of "A Letter" may refer to the death and funeral of Cunningham's mother. (The poem was first published the year after she died.) Regarding the sonnet, Cunningham once mentioned in conversation that when Harriet Monroe, the editor of *Poetry,* accepted the poem, she tried unsuccessfully to persuade him to capitalize the first letter of each line.

Sonnet on a Still Night

The brittle streets, with midnight walking flung
from curb to curb in rime-resounding fall,
now (pausing) still reverberate the tall
tension of the mind to friendship strung.

And over chimes that toll the twelve gone hours
from where the city lights its sky-hung pall,
your words, that speed pronouncement, shatter all
the twinging chill with noise like frozen flowers.

Oh, take the car, and coming to the city,
follow the head-waiter's evening smile;
glance quickly down the glass-reflecting aisle;
hang up your coat; then stretch your feet out straightly
and finger bread where there had been but lately
the far-heard chime of bells in sullen file.

(first published in *Poetry* 40 [April 1932])

With a Copy of Stevens' *Harmonium*

Receive a gift which more rewards myself
Since living in this verse you live in me,
Dazed with the mothless meaning of old lamps,
For I am more than half what I have read.
If gratitude so graciously becomes you,
Receive me also whom my hostage taught
His art of imprecise exactitude,
Ageless as that Passion the mass resumes
Though candles waste and rustle in the draft.
They shade your face with tongues of my desire.

You turn the pages and the choir intones,
Delicately discordant, tuned out of tune,
The Latin syllables to a Hartford pipe.
Pardon, Cecilia, that in your seasoned loft
Breathes from that "shouting Jesus" thing, Harmonium,
The Sunday Morning hymn of our unfaith.

Faith is the bony flame whose flesh we are,
As poets are the print that comprehends them.
Print eats the page like Alexandria's fire
Leaving the scant phrase no scholar may emend,
Yet here I found the unconjectured word,
And it is God, and it is one with you.

(first published in this form in *Hound and Horn* 7
[October–December 1933]; a slightly different
version of the poem appeared in *YSW* 4 [June 1933])

A Letter

A letter is the heart's good-will in brief,
But more than "yours sincerely" must be said;
Persuasive images induce belief
When fused with sure thought whereby feeling's led.

Thus you'll forgive me if I here relate
Facts that unformalized were meaningless:
That I stay home, drink coffee, sit up late,
With grudging hand apportioning excess,

Bent over the blear visions these have wrought,
Whose memoirs I outline with veinèd eye,
Making anatomies of mortal thought
Whose rich embodiment I must supply.

And when the eyes grow tired I slowly play
Rameau and Frescobaldi, Bull and Byrd;
If some few bars close to the music stay,
The twisted wheel of spinning Fate is heard,

Constrained, complete. And with this formal doom
The free imagination I involve,
Weave and unweave, Penelopeian loom
Whose pattern stays, the swift heart to resolve.

For in the shapeless vestiges of being,
The very agony of dying breath,
Beside whom we sit on with eyes unseeing,
There's that we cannot face, which we call death,

But, naming it, subdue it to our norm,
Made human by old symbols of man's worth,
By custom weathered in traditional form,
Till the clean house, the black hearse, the thrown earth,

Of one brief segment of eternity
Remain the several memories from what were.
They are not she nor what she meant to me,
But by this rosary I come to her,

Fingering the hard beads that shape the whole,
Though every tenth gives meditation pause,
And fancy from past insight draws the soul,
The assured effect of one primal cause.

Not otherwise, dear, do I come to you,
Not otherwise than to the type, the way,
Earthen image of the one God and true,
From where my hand and sentiment may stray

On the bare, marble surface of calm duty,
Unchanging real where the unreal may move
Through the firm patterns which reveal its beauty,
And in your beauty is concealed my love.

> (published in *Commonweal* 21 [April 12, 1935]; in 1937 in
> *Twelve Poets of the Pacific,* there appeared a version of this
> poem that dropped the first five stanzas and featured other,
> slighter revisions)

Appendix B

Cunningham's Versification

Cunningham cared a great deal about verse form. Though acknowledging that poetry has been characterized in many ways, he preferred to define it as "metrical composition" (*TPS,* 14) or as "metrical language" (*CE,* 256). In the realm of aesthetics, poetic structure represented for him the other, and as a working poet he had the same kind of respect for it that he had as a human being for other people. Metrical form was the extrapersonal element in composition, which he tried to reconcile and fuse with his personal experience. As he put it,

> to write is to confront one's primary experience with the externally objective: first, with the facts of experience and with the norms of possibility and probability of experience; secondly, with the objective commonality of language and literary forms. To be successful in this enterprise is to integrate the subjectively primary, the immediate, with the objectively communicable, the mediate, to the alternation of both by their conformation to each other. . . . It is the conquest of solipsism. (*CE,* 427)

And because Cunningham took this matter so seriously, it seems appropriate to say a few words about his versification.

Cunningham writes most of his poems in traditional iambic meters. These are measured, as Frost once observed, "so many feet to the line, seldom less than two or more than five in our language" (Richard Poirier and Mark Richardson, eds., *Robert Frost, Collected Poems, Prose, & Plays* [New York: Library of America, 1995], 847). Frost's observation well accords with Cunningham's practice. Generally, the shortest line he uses has two feet and four syllables, and the longest has five feet and ten syllables. We can illustrate the short two-foot measure—iambic dimeter—with the following lines. (Adopting the conventional method of scansion, we will let "x" stand for a metrically unstressed syllable, "/" for a metrically stressed syllable, and "|" for a division between feet.)

<pre>
   x   /   x /
Your book | affords
   x   /   x /
The peace | of art,
</pre>

```
  x   /     x    /
Within | whose boards
  x   /   x    /
The pas | sive heart . . .
```
                    ("Acknowledgement")

These lines illustrate the three-foot measure—iambic trimeter:

```
  x  /   x    /  x /
Alle | giance is | assigned
  x  /   x    /    x   /
Forev | er when | the mind . . .
```
                    ("Choice")

These illustrate the four-foot measure—iambic tetrameter:

```
  x   /      x /   x  /    x    /
The New | Reli | gion is | the True,
x   /    x  /   x  /   x  /
A trans | forma | tion o | verdue . . .
```
                    ("The True Religion")

And these illustrate the five-foot line—iambic pentameter:

```
  x    /    x   /    x  /   x  /    x  /
Life flows | to death | as riv | ers to | the sea,
  x   /   x   /   x    /    x  /   x   /
And life | is fresh | and death | is salt | to me.
```
                    ("Life flows to death")

Though the theoretical norm of iambic meter posits an absolutely regular alternation of light and heavy syllables, in actual practice the fluctuation is flexible and relative. It does not go kaBOOM, kaBOOM, kaBOOM. Sometimes the alternation is more pronounced, sometimes less. We can appreciate this point by supplementing the two-value system of conventional scansion with a four-level register that certain linguists have used, with 4 standing for heavy stress, 3 for secondary stress, 2 for tertiary stress, and 1 for weak stress. These distinctions are, it should be observed, nearly as rough-and-ready as those of the two-value system: living speech entails infinite gradations of stress that cannot be comprehended by any limited notational scheme. Further, especially in cases of syllables involving intermediate stress, different readers may hear different degrees of accent. Nevertheless, we can better suggest, with the four-level register, what actually happens in verse rhythm than we can with the two-value system.

```
I 4    I    2    I 4    I 2    I 4
x  /   x    /    x /   x /    x /
Distin | guished and | famil | iar, and | aloof
                    ("And what is love?")


I    4    I    4    3    4    I    4    I    4
x    /    x    /    x    /    x    /    x    /
They know | that wind | brings rain, | and rain | and wind
                    ("All Choice Is Error")


3    4    I    3    I 4    I 4    I 2
x  /  x    /    x /    x /    x /
Good For | tune, when | I hailed | her re | cently.
                    ("Good Fortune, when I hailed her")
```

In an iambic verse, then, the basic pattern of fluctuation is constant, but is continually modulated by the poet. It is continually modulated, for that matter, by language itself, because language consists of words of different lengths and shapes, and when these are set into the metrical grid they inevitably and variously vivify it.

To put the matter another way, Cunningham's versification involves, on the one hand, a fixed metrical norm and, on the other hand, variable speech rhythm. And these dual elements—meter and rhythm—operate concurrently. Availing ourselves of Duns Scotus's vocabulary, we might say that the distinction between meter and rhythm is merely "formal" (i.e., the qualities involved are distinguishable but not divisible) rather than "real" (i.e., the qualities are both distinguishable and discrete from one another). We can differentiate between meter and rhythm in analysis, but in practice they are inseparable. The general metrical essence and the particular rhythmical manifestation occur and are experienced simultaneously. The rhythmical haecceity of a verse line is embedded in its metrical archetype and vice versa. Every iambic pentameter manifests a "thisness" that makes it different from every other iambic pentameter; and every iambic pentameter (assuming it does not feature any of the metrical variations noted below) exhibits a universal pattern that makes it the same as every other iambic pentameter. In living verse, meter fuses with modulation and modulation with meter.

Modulation in Cunningham also results from the fact that he writes, as all good poets do, not only in feet, but also in phrases, clauses, and sentences. His lines sound different from one another on account of having different grammatical arrangements. A straightforward, balanced couplet like "Life Flows to Death" will sound one way, whereas the following couplet, with its fragmentary

sentence structure—and its first line running into the second—will sound an-
other way:

> Not, "Are you saved?" they ask, but in informal
> Insistent query, "Brother, are you normal?"
>
> > ("The Elders at their services")

This last couplet is additionally illustrative because it contains one of the two
common variations in iambic meters—an unaccented, hypermetrical syllable at
the end of the line (also called "a feminine ending"). That is, there is an extra,
metrically unstressed syllable beyond the meter:

> x /   x /   x /   x / x / (x)
> Not, "Are | you saved?" | they ask, | but in | informal
> x /   x   /   x   /   x /   x   / (x)
> Insis | tent quer | y, "Broth | er, are | you normal?"

The other common variation is a trochaic "substitution" at the beginning of
the line. Sometimes, that is, Cunningham will start a line with a trochee—a foot
consisting of a heavy syllable followed by a light one—rather than with an
iamb:

> / x   x /   x /
> Passion | is nev | er fact
>
> > ("Passion")

> / x   x   /   x/ x/   x /
> Reader, | it's time | real | ity | was faced
>
> > ("Reader, it's time")

Theoretically, substituted feet can occur anywhere in the line; however, the
only other place trochees appear with any frequency in iambic verse is after a
grammatical pause in the middle of a line. In the pentameter, this means in the
third or fourth foot:

> x / x   /   / x   x /   x /
> For we | are time, | monads | of pur | poses
>
> > ("Consolatio Nova")

Occasionally, we will find a line with all three variants just mentioned—the
trochaic first foot, the mid-line trochee, and the feminine ending. This occurs,
for instance, in opening verse of one of Cunningham's late epigrams:

```
/ x     x   /  x   /     /  x   x   / (x)
```
Busied | with priv | ate dreams, | earthen, | unspoken

("On Correggio's Leda")

Other wrinkles could be mentioned. Since the only requirement of an iambic foot is that the second syllable be heavier than the first, it is possible to follow a light iamb with a heavy iamb and produce four degrees of rising stress, as Cunningham does twice in this line:

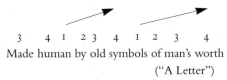

```
3    4  1  2 3   4   1  2   3    4
```
Made human by old symbols of man's worth

("A Letter")

Cunningham also makes use of a freedom historically allowed to poets: he treats contractible syllables as contracted or uncontracted as suits his metrical convenience. For example, in

```
x    /    >   / x  /
```
And stud | iously | amaze

("Hang up your weaponed wit")

he treats the "-ious" part of "studiously" as a single syllable. He treats the "i" as a consonantal "y." However, in

```
x    /   x  /   x  /  x/   x  /
```
Am con | stant and | invar | iant | by night

he does not contract "-iant" into "-yant," but gives each vowel full articulation. ("Elision" is the term that customarily refers to poetic contractions, and the many forms of these are discussed in brilliant if daunting detail by Robert Bridges in his *Milton's Prosody*.)

Because English speech naturally tends toward iambic rhythm, English poets, Cunningham included, use iambic meters more than any other. However, other meters, involving such rhythms as trochaic, dactylic, and anapestic, have been employed. And we occasionally find in Cunningham the most widely practiced non-iambic meter in English poetry, the trochaic tetrameter.

```
/  x    /  x    / x   / x
```
Under | neath this | pretty | cover
```
/  x   / x    / x   / x
```
Lies Van | essa's, | Stella's | lover.

```
  /   x   /   x    /    x    /  x
You that | under | take his | story
  /   x   /   x    /    x    /  x
For his | life nor | death be | sorry
   /   x   /  x    /    x     /[x]
Who the | abso | lute so | loved
   /  x    /  x    /  x     /  [x]
Motion | to its | zero | moved. . . .
```

("With a Copy of Swift's Works")

As the last couplet here indicates, poets working in trochaic lines, especially when they are rhyming them, sometimes drop the final syllable. The practice is termed "catalexis."

As the preceding remarks imply, traditional English verse counts and arranges both syllables and beats. However, English poets have experimented with meters based purely on accent-count; indeed, Old English verse and much Middle English verse is based primarily on accent, pointed and reinforced by alliteration. Likewise, English poets have on occasion experimented with a metric that entails only syllable-count. They also have sometimes imitated classical Greek and Latin meters. Cunningham tries his hand, at one time or another, at all of these variant forms. I indicate their occurrence in the notes to the poems in which he employs them.

The only common English metrical mode that Cunningham does not use is what Frost has called "loose iambic." This involves iambic rhythm varied by relatively frequent anapestic substitutions. It is customarily deployed in rhymed measures of less-than-pentameter length—the theory being that the rhymes and the comparative brevity of the lines are sufficient to maintain rhythmical integrity, despite the extra syllables produced by the anapests. Thomas Hardy's "In the Restaurant," William Butler Yeats's "Fiddler of Dooney," and Frost's "Neither Out Far Nor In Deep" exemplify this mode.

Index of Titles and First Lines

Page numbers in italics refer to the Commentary.